Becoming a Power Parent

Seven Guiding Principles for Creating a Healthy Family

by

Gary M. Barnard, Ph.D.

TELEMACHUS PRESS

This book is written for your personal entertainment. Because specific situations necessitate unique actions, before implementing any of the concepts discussed here in, please seek professional advice. Results will vary. No warranty, either expressed or implied, is made by the author or publisher.

If you purchased this book without a cover you should be aware that this book is stolen property. It was reported as "unsold and destroyed" to the publisher and neither the author nor the publisher has received any payment for this "stripped book."

BECOMING A POWER PARENT
Copyright © 2012 by GARY M BARNARD, Ph.D. All rights reserved, including the right to reproduce this book, or portions thereof, in any form. No part of this text may be reproduced, transmitted, downloaded, decompiled, reverse engineered, or stored in or introduced into any information storage and retrieval system, in any form or by any means, whether electronic or mechanical without the express written permission of the author. The scanning, uploading, and distribution of this book via the Internet or via any other means without the permission of the publisher is illegal and punishable by law. Please purchase only authorized electronic editions and do not participate in or encourage electronic piracy of copyrighted materials.

The publisher does not have any control over and does not assume any responsibility for author or third-party websites or their content.

Cover Art:
Copyright © Hemera/101031145/Thinkstock

Illustrator Ethan Ausburn

Published by Telemachus Press, LLC
http://www.telemachuspress.com

Visit the author website:
http://www.thepower-parent.com

Library of Congress Control Number: 2012956327

ISBN: 978-1-938701-62-7 (eBook)
ISBN: 978-1-938701-63-4 (Paperback)
ISBN: 978-1-939337-30-6 (Hardback)

Version 2012.12.27

Printed in the United States of America

10 9 8 7 6 5 4 3 2 1

Dedication

This book is dedicated to George and Bonnie Barnard who are my power parents, to Marialyn Price Barnard my co-power parent of 37 years, to Brandi Barnard Cone and Joshua Barnard my children who gave me the opportunity to become a power parent and to Wendell and Benjamin Cone, my grandchildren, who have expanded my role and my world with joy. You've all been patient and forgiving teachers as I've tried to be a worthy student.

Acknowledgments

Let me say a word of thanks to Leila Meacham, bestselling author of *Roses* and *Tumbleweeds* and my 10th grade English teacher. You've inspired me! You also introduced me to your copyeditor, Nancy. I'm indebted to you, Leila.

Many thanks go to Nancy Johanson, copyeditor extraordinaire. You were a tall drink of cool water on a *sizzlin* Texas summer day. Your patience and talent were always timely and so appreciated. Also, to all the staff at Telemachus Press … many thanks for your dedication to the success of this project.

To all of the families who allowed me to be part of your journey to health, well-being and peace, many times overcoming great odds, my deepest appreciation. You've taught me to never give up on the power of a parent.

To John Burnside, M.D., a steadfast friend and office partner for almost three decades. Thank you for your friendship and principled living.

Mentor and friend Roberto Jimenez, M.D.—your heart is bigger than Texas! You continue to show others that it is truly better to give than to receive.

Mom and Dad, you started all of this and have always been there for me. As a result, my journey has been wonderful. I am a grateful son.

To the best kids a dad could have, Brandi and Joshua, you were only occasionally my "Skinner Rats," but always my best teachers. You've provided me with the education I needed, when I needed it—along with a big scoop of humility. I'm a grateful dad.

To Wendell and Benjamin Cone, you brought back the joy of parenting ... part-time. You always bring a smile to my face and a very warm spot in my heart. I'm a grateful Grampy.

And lastly to Marialyn, you are "Sweeter than Tupelo honey, an Angel of the first degree," ~*Van Morrison*. Thank you for your perseverance in encouraging me to write this book. You always seem to believe in me even when I don't seem to believe in myself. Second only to God's grace, you are the best thing that has ever happened to me. I'm a grateful husband and partner.

Contents

Introduction	i
PART I: The Seven Principles	1
Chapter 1: Attachment Principle	3
Chapter 2: Autonomy Principle	17
Chapter 3: Balance Principle	25
Chapter 4: Bipolarity Principle	34
Chapter 5: Mutuality Principle	40
Chapter 6: Reinforcement Principle	46
Chapter 7: Parsimony Principle	56
PART II: Putting the Principles to Work	59
Chapter 8: The Starting Line	61
Chapter 9: The Power-Parent Skills	73
Chapter 10: The Principles of Development	98
Chapter 11: The Family Umbrella	110
Chapter 12: The Positive Opposite	122
Chapter 13: The Texas Three-Step	129
Chapter 14: The Hybrid	142
Chapter 15: One-Way Trip with Our Memories Meter Ticking	155
Epilogue	161
A Personal Message	173
Appendix	175

Foreword

There are good families and there are bad families. Families can range from the heavenly to the hellish. Dr. Barnard's book is about choosing to create a good family and how to keep it. I have been a family therapist for over 35 years. In all my work teaching, researching, studying and practicing, I have never come across such a jewel of a manual—original, clear, practical, yet so profound. Its beauty and strength stems from the author's creative use of the natural laws which govern life itself to building families as nature meant them to be—productive, healthy, wise and fun.

As I read and re-read *Becoming a Power Parent*, I discovered what a fool I have been all these years. The lessons since grade school to medical school, my training as a psychiatrist at Boston University and Harvard Medical Schools, my 40 years in teaching, research and practice—"there they were!" the laws of nature, jumping out of every sentence and page as they govern family systems. You can imagine how I felt. Why didn't I think about writing this book?

Now that I'm calmer and can set aside the propensities toward envy that too often characterize so many of us academics, I can truly say from the bottom of my heart, that *Becoming a Power Parent* is a gift to all of us who care about strong and healthy families. It is also a special gift for those families struggling to regain their creativity and strength from their current state of misfortune, no matter how dismal and hopeless our state may seem.

If I interpret Dr. Barnard's book accurately, it seems to me that his hope is to offer a framework to parents for understanding the natural laws that govern a family system and specific guidelines for conducting a successful family business. What is the business of a family? What are the essential ingredients of great parenting? How do leadership skills evolve within a family system? He attempts to tackle these vital and complex issues as he invites us to probe the obvious—the laws of nature.

We are not accustomed to look around us for solutions. The wisdom of the ancient world and the great spiritual masters throughout the ages knew how to look around them. Modern science has elaborated and clarified the laws of nature that govern all successful life as never before. Unfortunately, contemporary thinkers have relegated the laws of nature to the governance of life forms, not humanity. Humans, we are told, are free beings. We are free to govern ourselves as we see fit and according to our best interest. The laws of nature do not apply to us.

This revolutionary book, if I may call it that, clearly shows why modern family life has too often become such a messy business. If one ignores the laws of nature there will be negative consequences. "The laws of nature are clear and concise," states Dr. Barnard. They are universal and eternal. He shows us they accommodate the most complex, unimaginable and problematic family issues. They offer successful strategies for dealing with them. Understanding and allowing the natural laws that govern all life will lead to members of a family finding their ultimate purpose—a creative and fulfilling intimacy in their relationships with each other and with persons outside the family.

Becoming a Power Parent: Seven Guiding Principles for Creating a Healthy Family is a powerful book that should be read and studied by anyone concerned with the fate of family life—primarily by parents who desire to become powerful and effective leaders of their family. The book spells out a hopeful vision, if we develop respect and adhere to the natural laws that insure sturdy and healthy families. It presents an eloquent and beautiful argument for sacred truths—which we simply should not ignore. *Becoming a Power Parent* is intelligently written, warm, comforting, practical and rock solid. It will be especially helpful to us living in these complex and rapidly changing times.

Roberto L. Jimenez, M.D., F.A.P.A.
Adjunct Professor of Psychiatry
The University of Texas Health Science Center at San Antonio
Graduate—Boston Family Institute

Becoming a Power Parent

Introduction

WOULDN'T IT BE nice if there were a simple manual describing the basic principles for developing healthy children within a peaceful and productive family structure? You know, like an Owner's Manual. Perhaps we already have one.

The natural laws—meaning accepted, expected or innate rules or directives—used by healthy families are like the natural laws that regulate all life forms and systems. If we were asked, "What are the principles of life you most value?" we might say, "Freedom of choice, liberty, justice, sovereignty, peace of mind, or equality." These are all concepts of natural law. We believe they are our self-evident rights as human beings.

Even our youngest children know when something isn't fair. When visiting a public park, playground or community swimming pool where children are playing, we can observe their instant responses to unfairness. When a more aggressive or selfish child imposes his or her will upon one of the others—typically the perceived weakest—the mistreated child and others in the vicinity respond. They know instinctively what is right or just behavior. "Give me that ball! I want it!" is met with scowls, "No! It's mine!" or "You're not being nice!" Sometimes, the victim of the verbal assault cries out of a feeling of helplessness. The emotions prompted by an injustice affect a child's behavior and when our child hurts, we hurt as parents.

Although my training and practice as a behavioral scientist doesn't involve political science, I have found the laws of nature worthy of study and understanding. For instance, the power of these principles was drafted by Thomas Jefferson some 235 years ago in the words of the Declaration of Independence.

> We hold these truths to be self-evident, that all men are created equal, that they are endowed by their Creator with certain unalienable Rights, that among these are Life, Liberty, and the pursuit of Happiness. That to secure these rights, Governments are instituted among Men, deriving their just powers from the consent of the governed, that whenever any Form of Government becomes destructive of these ends, it is the Right of the People to alter or to abolish it, and to institute new Government, laying its foundation on such principles and organizing its powers in such form, as to them shall seem most likely to affect their Safety and Happiness.

This philosophy wasn't new in Jefferson's time. John Locke, a British empiricist in the 1600s, wrote a great deal about these natural principles.

We can apply the principles stated in the above quotation to those that allow us to think differently about our children and our family structure, by substituting Family(s) for Government(s), family for governed, and members for men.

> We hold these truths to be self-evident, that all *members* are created equal, that they are endowed by their Creator with certain unalienable Rights, that among these are Life,

Liberty, and the pursuit of Happiness. That to secure these rights, *Families* are instituted among *Members*, deriving their just powers from the consent of the *family*, that whenever any Form of *Family* becomes destructive of these ends, it is the Right of the *Members* to alter or to abolish it, and to institute new *Family*, laying its foundation on such principles and organizing its powers in such form, as to them shall seem most likely to affect their Safety and Happiness.

We are unaccustomed to thinking about our families in these terms. As parents, we have certain powers that are directly related to the natural principles that form the foundation of safety and happiness within our unit. *Becoming a Power Parent: Seven Guiding Principles for Creating a Healthy Family* is a hybrid of ideas from natural laws—which are self-evident, well-researched psychological principles of human behavior and from my experiences as a child psychologist in clinical practice for almost three decades. Its purpose is to present these ideas in a simple, concise, and meaningful way ... one that provides us with the knowledge and means to construct and develop—or deconstruct and redevelop—a family that understands and values safety, harmony, health, and happiness and can teach and perpetuate the positive results generation after generation.

We live in a complex and challenging world; technological advances have changed our ability as parents to limit or have knowledge of everything our children see, hear, read or experience and how they react to these stimuli. We need to become better trained and equipped to teach the value systems we hold dear and to show our children through example. If we fail in this mission, our children may, over time, intentionally or inadvertently "alter or abolish" what we currently experience as family. Someday, their new family units may be absent the principles that lead to the "Safety and Happiness" of their children ... our grandchildren.

Principles and Patterns

We all have beliefs that are products of our choices, intended and unintended. However, there are natural truths that don't need "belief" as a requisite for their existence. These natural principles exist independently and are intuitive, irrespective of our beliefs. They're Mother Nature's concepts; the most essential ones become *superordinate* (at the top of the list) and the less essential become *subordinate* (less important). For example, we can't live without oxygen; within six minutes, our brain cells begin to die. We can survive only 8-24 days without water, depending upon our age and physical condition, and how fast fluids leave our body (sweat, urine and tears), and only up to four weeks without food, again depending upon our weight, body temperature and our degree of physical exertion. We need all of these elements to live and thrive; however, the most essential is oxygen. It is at the top of nature's ladder. It is a superordinate concept.

Over the years, many people have believed they could fly. Whether they were under the influence of hallucinogens (drugs that caused changes in their thought processes), severely mentally ill (experiencing a psychotic break from reality), or merely convinced they had special powers, all met the same fate as they leaped from a very tall structure. They hit the ground at the same speed and their direction was only downward, never up into the clear blue sky. The superordinate principle of Mother Nature in this scenario is gravity. Believe what we will, nature's reality is what counts. The clear and instinctive principle of gravity is a great teacher. Gravity is predictable, and therefore, reliable. There's no emotional or punitive meaning behind it. We must all accept this principle, because it's provable.

The bottom line is that most of us will adjust our beliefs to match this simple principle, once we're shown proof of its claim. We call this process "learning" or a "pattern shift."

"That's just not true!" some of us are wont to protest. "What about people flying in airplanes or gliders or when they jump out of airplanes with parachutes?" Exactly! Now we're using our powers of reasoning. Just because a principle is true and instinctive doesn't mean it can't be integrated with others. That's precisely how creative people who observed and thought about gravity integrated it into the principles of aerodynamics and thermodynamics to enable us to fly. As we learn about nature's principles and understand how they predictably interact with each other, we can make healthy shifts in our own. We call this having "adaptability."

There is a well-known story often used to describe this interesting relationship between principles and patterns. Stephen Covey, a best-selling author recognized as one of *Time* magazine's 25 most influential Americans, used it in his renowned book, *The Seven Habits of Highly Effective People*. Max Lucado, a San Antonio minister and author of over 60 books (65 million sold worldwide), used it in his best seller, *In the Eye of the Storm*. The story hasn't been confirmed as factual and it has likely changed considerably over the years, but it nicely illustrates the purpose of our undertaking.

> One particular night, a ship's progress was being hindered by a thick and patchy fog. Deeply concerned, the captain was on duty with his crew. Suddenly, the loud voice of the lookout broke the silence.
>
> "Captain, light bearing on the starboard bow!"
>
> "Is it steady or moving astern?" the captain called out.
>
> "Steady, captain."
>
> The captain then called to the signalman, "Signal that ship. Tell it we are on a collision course and advise it to change its course 20 degrees."
>
> Back came a signal. "Advisable for you to change your course 20 degrees."

The captain stiffened. "Send this. I am Captain; change course 20 degrees."

"I am Seaman Second Class," came the reply. "You had better change course 20 degrees."

By now, the captain was furious. He barked off another order. "I am a battleship. Change course 20 degrees!"

Back came the quick reply, "I am a lighthouse. Still advise you to change course 20 degrees."

Guess who changed?

Principles have solid foundations and are real. They don't change. It is our pattern or standard that needs to adjust and be realigned with what is real. If not, there are usually very clear, predictable, and undesirable consequences to follow.

Aristotle claimed that the heavier an object, the faster it would fall to the ground. For centuries, people believed he was right. Why not? His name was used much like we use Einstein's name today. He was admired for being bright and a great thinker. However, this was an observable natural principle that anyone could have tested to determine its truth. No one did.

Some 2,000 years later, a fellow by the name of Galileo staged a public experiment off the Leaning Tower of Pisa. He called a few of the leading scholars and professor-types of the time to observe it. With all eyes on him, he proceeded to drop both a ten-pound and a one-pound weight from the top of the tower at the identical time. Both weights hit the ground at precisely the same instant. This was astounding proof. It completely refuted the long-held theory. Finally, someone's curiosity had advanced to the point of taking action. It made no difference to the learned men who monitored Galileo's experiment. The long-held and accepted paradigm was so powerful, they denied what they saw with their own eyes and continued to believe Aristotle's hypothesis. Unfortunately, many of us live with our own erroneous beliefs, even in the face of indisputable evidence to the contrary.

Perhaps it's finally time to base our pattern of parenting and family on a few natural and simple truths. Certain fundamental principles are effectively connected to healthy and peaceful living. As parents, we have the potential to become the most powerful agents of change and reform. We can decide to do nothing, or we can decide to make whatever adjustments are necessary to lead toward the making of more successful, safe, and happy children within our healthy family unit. But, how do we go about doing this?

Becoming a Power Parent: Seven Guiding Principles for Creating a Healthy Family is written for the express purpose of helping every concerned parent or potential parent with this mission. Our children, and perhaps our civilization as we know it, depend on our getting it right.

The Epilogue provides a "bullet-point" review of each chapter. Refer to it as you need. Also, note that the book is presented in two parts: Part I—The Principles, and Part II—Putting the Principles to Work. While I hope you enjoy the book, my greatest hope is that it helps you achieve your parenting goals while finding joy and peace in healthy family living.

—Gary M. Barnard (Dr. B)

PART I
The Seven Principles

Chapter 1
Attachment Principle

A slender acquaintance with the world must convince every man that actions, not words, are the true criterion of the attachment of friends.
~George Washington (1732–1799)

GEORGE WASHINGTON RECOGNIZED that our pattern of behaviors (how we regularly choose to act) is primarily responsible for our attachments to others. Most of us do have "A slender acquaintance with the world," consequently; we have a general sense of how we connect to our children. While this seems intuitive, and therefore apparent, I ask you to bear with me in this first chapter as I share somewhat technical information that can help you view this "attachment principle" in a different, and perhaps a more powerful, way than you do currently. This is the beginning principle for the *Power Parent*. It is the hinge pin that holds it all together.

This chapter is a bit longer than some of the other chapters, and I admit that because I have included more technical information it reads more like a text book than I prefer (my apologies). Let me encourage you to read, re-read and fight through this chapter, if that is what it takes. Skip around. Come back to it after you have read most or the entire book. There are some profound mysteries related to early attachment that can only be understood by working through the process.

Okay, deep breathing ... good. Here's the preview. Our objectives for this chapter are to gain an understanding that:

- The parent-child attachment process is natural, follows certain rules and begins day-one with our newborn child.
- We parents are in charge of bonding with our children and we must choose behaviors that will encourage their attachment to us.
- We must balance our behaviors with developing a secure base and encouraging safe self-exploration. Our "internal working model" expresses our own pattern of attachment and this can predict that of our children.
- We are the primary teachers of our children. Their secure attachment to us helps them learn more efficiently.
- All of the effective daily management of our family environment and family relationship is hinged to the attachment principle and promotes cooperation (team work) within a healthy family unit.
- Attachment is the first principle of the Power Parent.

After WW II, when children were left homeless and orphaned, a well-known psychiatrist noticed the increased presence of significant difficulties in these children's lives. The United Nations asked him to write a document describing his observations. He did so, and in the years to come also published a three-volume study, *Attachment and Loss* (1969-1982), which offered a more detailed and comprehensive report of his research and that of several others, related to attachment theory. The Attachment Principle, for our purpose, can be formally defined as the natural tendency for a connection to be formed whenever an organized set of behaviors is consistently part of the social interaction between our children and our self.

For us parents, the common sense and practical understanding of this interaction is the well-known bond that usually occurs between a mother and her infant. Part of this principle seems to be instinctive, but part is acquired and developed through learning and reinforcement.

During the same time period, a well-known developmental psychologist further defined three attachment patterns with her research, with a fourth added as additional research indicated: secure attachment, avoidant attachment, ambivalent/anxious or resistant attachment and disorganized attachment. She also coined the term "secure base" or "secure haven" and described it as *rapprochement,* which is French for "bring together." In other words, if our children have a secure attachment with us from the time of their birth, they are more likely to explore and learn about their environment when they have the knowledge of a *secure base* to return to, especially in times of need.

In the context of this attachment theory, we're speaking about an affectionate bond between our children and their attachment figures, who are usually "us" their parents. Our children's need for protection, security and safety instinctively motivates such a connection. The psychological aim is security and the biological aim is survival. Over time, our infant and toddler children can seek closeness and attachment with more than one person and will start to discriminate between several caregivers and arrange a hierarchy, with the principal caregiver at the top. This is usually the mother, but can be the father or grandparent or any individual who is sensitive and responsive in social interactions. As our children mature and are confronted with greater demands in a larger world, they become more discriminative and flexible in the use of their attachment hierarchy.

On The Lighter Side

In the American television comedy *Modern Family*, Claire and Phil Dunphy have three children: Haley (17), Alex (14), and Luke (11). The regular viewer of this weekly series knows that each child has a pretty secure attachment with each parent. With a pre-teen boy and two teenage girls, however, drama and excitement are right around the corner.

In one particular episode, the writers depict how the hierarchy of attachment can be rather flexible, depending on the role played by the parent and the needs (or perceived needs) of the children. Every family has recognizable patterns of co-existence. Claire was being the "bad cop," but she had reached her limit. She wanted to be the fun parent, so she told Phil to take over the role of the disciplinarian with the two older daughters. Phil had planned to take Luke and his cousin Manny on an outing to ride go-carts, but Claire took over that activity and demanded that he deal with Haley and Alex, who were planning to go to the Movie Theater and then shop. His marching order was to tell them they could not leave the house until their shared bathroom was completely cleaned. The girls knew that Dad was the easily swayed one who had no spine when it came to saying "no" to fun. They scurried up the stairs, made a half-hearted effort to throw all of their toiletries into a cabinet, and then attempted a quick get-a-way.

When Dad saw the results of their puny efforts, he was incensed. The next scene showed him jumping on the car hood to stop his girls from escaping their responsibilities. Taking on a rather maniacal disciplinarian role, he cancelled their outing and ordered them to clean for the rest of the day without eating. At the same time this was unfolding, Claire was equally maniacal in her attempt to be "fun" with Luke and Manny. She was so determined to be a "cool" parent that she not only let them do and eat whatever they wanted, she also pressured them to keep up with her hypomanic pace. The end result was a scene with Luke throwing up in Claire's car because he had eaten too much.

One of the points of this humorous portrayal is to illustrate how children learn to use their hierarchy of attachments to get what they want. This working of the parents against each other is called *splitting*, and at times it does seem amusing and harmless, as in this case with Phil and Claire. They came to the realization that changing their roles in such an extreme way could cause ambivalence and disorganization in their attachments with their kids (not to mention the exhaustion that comes from such an experiment). Consequently, they easily slid back into their comfortable and seemingly manageable roles. Without recognition of the disorganization and the ability to use effective and predictable behaviors of secure attachment, however, children and families are headed for trouble.

Parent Bonds—Child Attaches

In a child-to-adult relationship, the child's connection is called the *attachment* and the adult's connection is called the *bond*. As parents, we bond emotionally and behaviorally with our children from the time they are infants, and because we're available for consistent and caring responsiveness to their needs; we become their *attachment figures*. Research suggests that while proximity and quantity of interaction have a role, the quality of our interaction is more important. This means that we, as parents, must have a specific set of behaviors. These behaviors involve engaging in lively social interaction with our children from an early age and responding readily and effectively to their signals and approaches. We must be physically and emotionally available and fully engaged, for healthy bonding-attachment to develop. Our sensitivity and our involvement seem to be the important factors that we control.

The goal of the attachment behavioral system is for us to ensure that our children maintain a connection with an available and accessible attachment figure. They are more likely to become alarmed when fearful of danger or anxious when afraid of being cut off from us. But as they develop strong and secure attachments, the level and frequency of their alarm and anxiety tend to diminish, thus allowing more exploration.

Text Book Alert!!!

A table in the Appendix shows the four attachment patterns and the associated characteristic patterns of behaviors from previously mentioned research (if you are interested).

Infants can form attachments even if they're mistreated by their caregiver. The quality of the attachment, however, depends on the history of their care, as they begin to predict the behavior of their caregiver through repeated interactions. The focus is the organization or pattern of the interaction and not, necessarily, the quantity of attachment behaviors. The goal is to form a secure attachment pattern, because an *in*secure pattern tends to disrupt exploration, self-confidence and mastery of their environment, leading to eventual problems with their gaining independence. Young children are more likely to explore when their caregiver is present. The bottom line, then, is that the attachment our infants develop with us depends on the *quality* of care we provide for them. We need to be present and engaged in our children's lives as we expose them to an enriched environment, and then enjoy them as they explore and develop confidence. Even more basically, we must teach them they can trust us to meet their every need in a sensitive and caring way.

Psychological Needs May Trump Biological Needs

Another well-known psychologist conducted two attachment studies involving infant rhesus monkeys (sometimes my kids acted like little monkeys). He found that the primary attribute of a surrogate mother was not the provision of food, but rather "softness." These infant monkeys formed an affectionate bond with a soft object that didn't provide food and was pleasant to touch, and not with a wire object that was unpleasant to touch but did provide food. Biological survival requires nourishment, right? We would predict, therefore, that food would be at the top of the infant's hierarchy, but softness—a psychological need—seemed to play a stronger role in attachment. Our lesson from these studies is that, as parents, we need to provide plenty of affectionate and tender touch for our children as we help them develop a secure base.

Interesting Statistics

Approximately 65 percent of children in the general population are classified as having a secure pattern of attachment. That leaves 35 percent with an insecure attachment divided across the remaining three patterns. Child development researchers in the 1990s studied the extent to which parental attachment predicts their children's classification pattern. It appears that about 75 percent of the time, the parents' perception (internal working model) of their own childhood attachments was found to predict their children's pattern. Knowing this, we can change the way in which we relate to our children to ensure we develop a close bond with each one.

Patterns tend to vary with the degree of stability in the caregiving conditions over the long term. As our children's conditions change—because of stress from family poverty, illness, divorce, death, verbal abuse or feelings of abandonment—their pattern of attachment will also vary from secure to insecure. As well-informed parents, we can make the necessary responses to these stressors and minimize the disruptive and altering patterns. We can fully understand why children who have been physically abused or neglected have a high probability for developing *insecure* attachments and why they're also likely to remain in that classification pattern throughout their pre-school years. Neglect alone dramatically increases the likelihood of developing insecure attachments.

Secure Or Insecure Attachments—*Your* Choice

There is a considerable body of research that demonstrates an association between attachment organizations and our children's ability to function across multiple areas. The studies suggest that compared to securely attached children, the adjustment of insecure children is not as soundly regulated and places them at higher risk for poor relationships in the future. There are many factors that influence social know-how, but it appears that secure infants are more likely to become socially competent than their insecure peers. We need to be aware, however, that once our children reach the age of attending nursery or grade school, their peer relationships greatly influence the development of their social skills, cognitive development, and the formation of their social identity, which takes on added importance in their adolescent years.

Our children's social adjustment has been accurately predicted by the classification of their peer status (popular, neglected or rejected). Insecure children—especially avoidant children—are particularly vulnerable. As common sense would predict, their social and behavioral difficulties tend to wax and wane with the deterioration or improvement in the quality of the parenting they receive. If our children acquire an early secure attachment to us as their caregivers, this bond seems to have a long-term protective function in their healthy social development. We may not be able to control all future events that will be stressful for them, but doing our part to smooth the progress of the attachment-bond with them, as their secure base, will go a long way in helping them flourish with security, leading to adaptive autonomy.

Of all the patterns of attachment, it seems that the most concerning is the disorganized classification. In notable studies, the statistical probability that *"mistreated children"* will be classified in this pattern is 80 percent. Only about 12 percent of the non-abused sample of children was classified as disorganized. It's interesting to note that approximately the same percentage of non-abused children who had the disorganized pattern (12 percent) was also found in the abused sample to have the secure pattern (15 percent). Obviously, there are other internal and external factors influencing attachment patterns. Again, common sense suggests that some of those factors are individual biological and psychological differences and some are based on other relationships, such as those with another parent (stepparent), nanny, day care provider, and other relatives.

Highest Risk!
To summarize, a child with an insecure pattern of attachment (particularly disorganized) is at high risk for future childhood disorders. While research doesn't link this pattern to the cause of a *specific disorder*, it does establish the connection with a much higher risk for peer relationship problems, including increased anxiety, mood regulation problems, and disruptive behavior. For example, in a school setting, an anxious child is more likely to have internalized problems and be moody or depressed, or to experience increased body complaints and withdrawal. An avoidant and disorganized child is more likely to develop externalized problems and be more aggressive or defiant and exhibit other conduct disturbances.

The attachment process might be understood best as an "attachment behavior system." No parent has always behaved in an ideal way to promote perfect bonding and attachment. This fact is not to excuse us, but rather to explain the importance of our developing a healthy and adaptive model or pattern.

Based on past philosophical and theoretical writings, but especially on more current cognitive psychological research, we know that an "internal working model" has much to say about attachment and our relationships. Internal working models are an association of mental pictures and aroused feelings. These mechanisms give us the ability to anticipate and interpret another person's behavior and then plan an appropriate response. As we physically grow and mature, we have a greater sophistication in our model. Research suggests that our brains don't fully mature until we're in our mid-twenties or later. As parents, then, we have the ability to reflect on our internal working model related to attachment and to make whatever changes are necessary for the sake of our children. We'll want to do this, because of the evidence that our children's attachment pattern is predicted by our own attachment pattern.

Positive Self-Image

If our infants and toddlers experience security, support, and encouragement from us, as their primary caretakers, they're more likely to develop a positive self-image and then expect positive behaviors from others. On the other hand, if they experience neglect and abuse, they're more likely to develop a negative self-image and then project the same negative characteristics onto others.

Studies show that these models have continued across three generations. Who we are and what we do has a lasting impact on our children, grandchildren and great-grandchildren. If our children fall into the same categories as our own, then, as parents, our internal working model governs the way we relate to them. Some experts believe that the earliest internal working models formed are the most likely to persist, because they're deeply embedded in the subconscious. However, our working models are subject to change, depending on our experiences and our own personal responsibility for adaptive change.

Will They Ever Sleep Through The Night?

Let's think about a practical example ... one that involves the sleep behavior of our infants and toddlers. All of us have experienced the difficulty of training them to fall readily asleep and learning how to initiate sleep by themselves when they awaken during the night. We worked hard to develop routines for feeding, rocking, and comforting them, in an effort to help them develop good sleeping habits. Some of us failed, because we didn't know how to go about it. Our guilt kept us running back to the nursery every time our child cried and they quickly learned that crying ultimately brings comfort.

Studies have demonstrated ways to balance the task of being the secure base and encouraging our children to develop internal mechanisms of comfort. One such study filmed the parents and their child during a several-night experiment. Essentially, the parents were instructed to wait patiently in their bed when they heard their child crying, up to 15 minutes. During the first night, the parents were visibly nervous and upset. This waiting period was likely more traumatic for them than for their child, who was crying loudly and continuously in the next room. The parents were instructed to go to the child's room and speak softly and gently, while caressing and patting the child's back. No picking up to comfort. After a short period of time, they were to retreat to their own room and wait for another 15 minutes before repeating the same routine (… the pain of it all!). As you can imagine, this was a trying time, with one result being sleep deprivation for the parents.

However, there was another interesting result unfolding in the next room. Their child was experimenting with self-comforting or self-regulating behaviors, including the well-known rooting behavior associated with discharging tension. Their child was also using the tactile stimulation of a soft blanket for soothing, and making a noticeable effort to "nest" or find a secure and comfortable corner in the crib. As these behaviors became more organized, the crying subsided and sleep was not only initiated in short order, but was maintained. Back in the other room, the parents were comfortably sleeping through the rest of night.

It seems that when we are bonded with our children, and we engage in an organized and adaptive pattern of behavior, they are able to develop secure attachment, balance and autonomy (self-regulation). Our conscious efforts promote healthy systems for our family's growth. This bonding and healthy and secure attachment is a natural mechanism that will affect many aspects of our children's lives. One of the aspects will be our strong parent-child relationship and its association with their behavior management.

In simple terms, what can we take away from this first principle of attachment?

- The parent-child attachment process is natural and follows certain rules. It begins from the moment our children are born into this world.
- We parents are in charge of emotionally bonding with our children and we must choose to behave in an organized and predictable manner, if our children are to learn how to develop a secure attachment. The process takes work and will require our availability and accessibility for our children.
- We must balance our behaviors with developing a secure base and encouraging safe self-exploration. Recognizing and developing sophistication with our own internal working model is an immense help in the attachment process, as our working model expresses our own pattern of attachment and this can predict that of our children.
- We are the primary teachers of our children. When they are securely attached to us, their learning becomes more expansive and efficient.
- All of the effective daily management of our family environment and family relationship is hinged to the attachment principle. Because we are securely connected, we have a great deal to loose. Hence, we have greater motivation to cooperate and remain connected as a healthy family.
- Attachment is the first principle of the Power Parent.

If you are saying to yourself, "I really dropped the ball on the attachment principle," please don't despair and give up. Now is a great time to change and establish behavioral patterns that encourage your children to view you as a secure and trusted base.

Chapter 2
Autonomy Principle

In ourselves
In our own honest hearts and chainless hands
Will be our safeguard:
Nevermore
Let the great interest of the State depend
Upon the thousand chances that may sway
A piece of human frailty; swear to me
That ye will seek hereafter in yourselves
The means of sovereignty.
–Ion. Act V, Sir Thomas Noon Talfourd (1795–1854)

SIR TALFOURD NAILED it in Act V of his play. All groups only remain healthy when, "In our own honest hearts and chainless hands" (truth and liberty) we remain sovereign individuals. The Autonomy Principle is the natural law of sovereignty, meaning "supreme power." As human beings, we are all created equal with the free will to make choices. This freedom is our highest power and it's at the core of our very existence. Especially in democratic countries, we citizens are often willing to fight or die for this sovereign right. We place a high value on it. Not because we are better than anyone else, but because this is our God-given right and is necessary for health and happiness. With this right, however, comes an associated and hefty price—personal responsibility for the outcome of our choices.

What A Mess!
Choices bring consequences. For instance, if we spill our milk, we must clean it up. It doesn't mean we are stupid or bad or that we should be punished for spilling the milk. It simply means we must take the time and energy required to clean up the mess we've made. If we continue to go around spilling milk on a frequent basis, it may begin to define us as being inefficient and without the ability to adapt. Since we're likely to reject that characterization, we learn how to pay attention and be more careful when drinking milk. Our effective teacher, in this case, is the natural principle, not emotionally punitive consequences from a third party.

If we get to make choices, then everyone else gets to make them, too. That's fair. If we don't believe and support this, we're hypocrites. We're just entitled actors who pretend to live by principles when they work in our favor, while not extending this same right to everyone around us—others who may accuse us of being unjust and unreasonable. What makes us equal is that each of us has the right to make choices, not that we are all the same in other ways.

The Autonomy Principle is a natural and self-evident law. The only way we're not autonomous (independent; self-governing) is if we give up our right to make choices or allow others to take away our free will. This principle is true for us as parents and equally true for our children.

Are You Kidding?

Wait a minute. As we think about this, we may find ourselves becoming uncertain or ready to challenge the very thought of such a bold statement. It affects our current belief about the parent-child relationship. We have long-held viewpoints about our role, not unlike those people had for centuries about Aristotle's theory that something bigger and heavier falls faster than something smaller and lighter. As parents, we're accustomed to thinking we're older and wiser and more experienced; therefore, we have the right to decide on every issue. Children are to be seen and not heard. Children are to listen and watch and learn ... and obey.

Our children have just as much right to choice—their free will—as we do. But, how do we honor their right to choose while keeping them safe and, at the same time, clearly present to them our value system? When they're very young, we can take this right of theirs away from them, and we do when we deem it necessary for their safety. However, if we routinely dishonor their right to choose, this may be quite damaging to their health and well-being. It's a natural right, because it's a built-in principle that's necessary for their healthy and independent development and functioning. If we remove their right to choose, and they don't develop the ability to make good choices, they may depend on someone else to choose for them throughout their lifetime or continue to make poor choices.

Ahhhh ... Isn't That Sweet

Without free choice, everything changes. Let's consider more deeply the parent-child relationship. When we ask our children to give us a hug and they choose to do so, it feels good because they chose to comply. But, is there a change in our experience when, unprompted, our child voluntarily hugs us? The answer is likely, "Yes." We give that experience a different meaning. After multiple experiences of prompting and modeling affection with our children, there is a shift in their pattern so that choosing to offer us affection is a sign of their love. The consequence has a stronger connection with us. The strengthening of this connection provides safety, security, and trust and can eventually lead to interdependency. That's the way love and secure attachment works ... by choice.

On the other hand, we must use our common sense and intervene when our children are in danger. There are very clear times in their lives that natural consequences are simply unacceptable within our value system. Consider the sensitive and emotionally charged topic of suicide. Even though free societies accept the sovereignty of individual humans, including our children, we simply do not allow this choice if we can help it. Our civil laws in the United States have built-in provisions for removing this right and forcing protection and treatment on anyone who is in imminent danger of harming him/herself or others.

Another example that brings a fear response to any parent is that of a child playing in the street. The natural consequence of allowing them to learn by getting hit by a vehicle is absurd. What we may do is use logical consequences that will teach our children the rule of "no playing in the street." There will be more discussion of logical consequences in a later chapter.

To live successfully by this principle of autonomy, we must challenge our pattern of thinking and that of those with whom we hope to have a close relationship and make shifts that reflect the true nature of the principle. The reason we extend free choice to people in our life (including our children) is because they are sovereign and have supreme power, just like us. It's right and just, and this is the way we function best. To develop their highest power, our children must learn how to do things for themselves. If we can guide them to this end, we are successful parents. Our mantra, in this case, becomes: Help them do it by themselves.

The Lighthouse And The Seagull
Another story about a lighthouse is useful in our discussion (okay ... so I like lighthouses). It goes like this:

> Near an outcropping of majestic seaside cliffs, a lighthouse stood tall and steadfast. Its light alerted ships of the rocky terrain ahead. It informed those who saw its light shining through the darkness of their current position and guided them to safety.
>
> Certainly such a lighthouse would beam its radiant beacon assuredly and confidently from its very first day. Not this particular lighthouse. During the first days, the sun illuminated its environment of perilous cliffs and treacherous rocks. When confronted by the driving rain and winds, dense fog and haze of storms, especially during the darkness of nighttime danger, this lighthouse would invariably become frightened.
>
> One day, a seagull perched on the rim of its highest peak and commented on the sense of fear and sadness displayed by the lighthouse. "I'm afraid of the storms and the rain, the wind and the fog," the lighthouse confessed. "At night, I'm engulfed in darkness, and during the day, I'm surrounded by perilous cliffs and treacherous rocks."
>
> "But, you're a lighthouse," the seagull said. "Your strength can withstand the strongest storms. Your light beams through the darkness. You're sturdy and steadfast and the rocks and cliffs pose no threat to you."

"Yes, but I see the ships in the ocean tossing and turning in the churning waters of the stormy sea," the lighthouse lamented. "I see the cliffs and rocks veiled in the storms and fog, masked in the darkness of night. I may not be in danger, but I fear for the safety of the ships. They face real hazards and death-defying danger. I just stand here beaming my light. I want to stop the storms. I want to clear the fog and move the rocks and cliffs. I want to illuminate the darkness as brightly as a sunny day, but I can't even do that. I can't offer enough light to provide clear visibility. I can only produce a narrow beam. I feel I'm not doing enough and I'm frustrated, because I can't do more to help."

The seagull thought for a moment. "You're just a lighthouse. You can't clear the weather or completely illuminate the darkness, and you certainly can't move giant rocks or cliffs. Lighthouses don't have these powers. You underestimate the power of your light, however. You stand in hazardous surroundings and in the midst of storms and darkness. Your beacon is a steadfast signal of hope and safety. Have you considered how ships see you? When your beacon cuts through the storm, it says, 'Danger lies here. Navigate carefully.' What would happen if you weren't here?"

The lighthouse contemplated the seagull's words and finally rejoiced in a better understanding of its function and limited abilities. It stood tall and resolute and fulfilled its appointed duty, without fear and without lamenting its limitations. ~Author unknown

Be *Your* Child's Lighthouse

As parents, we are our children's lighthouse. Our role is to empower them with the ability to navigate themselves safely through the storms and confusion and temptations that could cause them to trip and fall. We do this through the steadfast strength of our interminable beacon, which represents their inspiration, encouragement and symbol of hope.

While we may readily accept the example of ourselves as a lighthouse for our children, we may still hesitate to make an aligning shift in our pattern of thinking and behaving. We have been taught to believe we must make choices *for* our children, even after they have reached adulthood. Truthfully, we must teach them to do most tasks for themselves, based upon choices *they* make. As we successfully make this change in our parenting methods, our fears and worry about encouraging the right of free choice will subside. We will experience genuine excitement in the acceptance of our parenting power and be able to focus on what we *can* do, rather than on what we *cannot* do. We will be able to stand strong and steadfast and calm, even in the midst of family trials and tribulations. What an incredibly potent way to empower our children with autonomy.

As long as we are "beaming" encouragement and hope and not attempting to usurp the responsibilities of our children, they will learn how our principled parenting methods can positively influence their choices now and in the future. Choice is central to living healthy, purposeful, and independent lives. If we embrace choice in our own lives and extend it freely to our children, they will acquire more experience with the outcomes of their choices within the safe laboratory of our family unit.

Choice is our highest individual right. It is our responsibility and only ours to claim and exercise it. Choice is the very foundation of our freedom as a human being. To be proactive as a power parent, we must first value and respect it as an autonomy principle, and then pass on this priceless self-governing right to our children.

Chapter 3
Balance Principle

Blessing on him who invented sleep, the mantle that covers all human thoughts, the food that appeases hunger, the drink that quenches thirst, the fire that warms the cold, the cold that moderates heat, and lastly, the general coin that purchases all things, the balance and weight that equals the shepherd with the king, and the simple with the wise. ~Miguel de Cervantes Saavedra (1547–1616)

BALANCE IS A pervasive principle in our daily lives. We see and feel it at work everywhere. After a busy and often hectic day, we need sleep to bring our bodies back into balance. There are several other natural mechanisms, in addition to sleep, that create the equilibrium we require to face another day of challenges with enthusiasm.

A biological term for this concept is *homeostasis* or homeostatic regulation, which is one of nature's finest principles. Without homeostasis working smoothly and automatically, the many different organs and systems in our bodies would undergo such chaos, we couldn't survive. Our hormones, blood sugar, electrolyte system, oxygen level, and body temperature, for instance, must all remain stable and balanced, or we suffer a biological crisis.

The natural principle of balance is also necessary in our holistic everyday life. The ways we think, feel and behave are critically linked to it.

Oh No! Not Math

In mathematics, there's a phenomenon in statistical analysis known as "regression to the mean," which simply means a movement back to the mathematical "average" or the middle. We can describe this process, which uses the principle of balance, with an example relating to height in humans. While it's true that people worldwide are becoming taller, it's a stabilized growth over time. In order for this change to occur, shorter people must have a tendency to have taller children, and taller people must have a tendency to have shorter children. That allows for the average height of humans to remain fairly stable.

First Math, Now Biology ... Are You Nuts?

This balance principle is also related to adaptation. Again, we'll use an example related to how our bodies function without our conscious input. Even though our core body temperature is, on the average, 98.6 degrees, we're able to adapt to changes in external or ambient temperature because of homeostatic regulation (balance). If we exercise too strenuously or if we have a fever, our core temperature may rise two or three degrees, sometimes causing a heat stroke. If we're exposed to extreme cold for a lengthy period of time without the proper clothing protection, we may become susceptible to hypothermia. While both of these are life-threatening, homeostasis, one of the main functions of our hypothalamus gland, works hard to maintain our body's status quo and return it to its normal temperature. It's such an elegant and essential principle; yet, we take this balance necessity for granted. We expect our body to make the required adjustment and rarely give it a passing thought.

Do you remember the earlier story about Aristotle and Galileo in the introduction? It took 2,000 years before Galileo came along and publicly challenged the conventional wisdom about the speed of mass within the earth's gravity. Even after he supplied indisputable evidence, the scholars of the time denied it. It has been theorized that one explanation for this kind of unreasonable denial is homeostasis.

Physics Too ... Natural Principles are Everywhere

We can think of the denial of obvious truth as an opposing force or resistance to whatever is a natural occurrence. Let's use the example of a river. Rivers always flow downhill, and most begin high up in the mountain with the melting of snow. Along the way to the sea, these rivulets collect additional water from rain and springs and other streams, increasing the flow into valleys and basins. We can try to control this rapidly increasing flow of water by building a dam to store the water in a lake, but what happens when heavier than usual snow melts and more frequent and uncharacteristically strong spring rains produce an even greater flow resulting in a massive and pervasive flood? The water will find a natural way around and over this dam and cause devastation to the areas downstream. Water takes the path of least resistance and can become a mighty force to reckon with.

What do we do about this phenomenon of nature, when the lives of humans are in potential danger? We commission engineers to build a higher and wider dam in an effort to resist the flow of the water and control nature. Sometimes this works, other times not. Or, we have the engineers install a steel gate at the base of the dam that can be opened and closed through a valve system, in an attempt to regulate the resistance. As the flood waters descend from the mountains, the same amount that comes into the lake is released downstream in a regular or balanced manner. The water automatically flows through the valve when the gate is opened, because the cavity provides a place of least resistance. This is a natural way to help the volume of water remain balanced.

When those early scientists resisted or denied the natural truth that a ten-pound and one-pound weight falls to the ground at the same speed, they were attempting to control natural laws. They had invested so much of their own thinking into Aristotle's belief that they couldn't accept the natural truth revealed in Galileo's demonstration. In their endeavor to keep everything as it had always been, they were essentially "building the dam higher and wider to control the flow of the water." This kind of resistance to truth distorts nature's mechanisms for maintaining regularity or balance.

Okay ... Get to the Point

What has all this discussion of balance in nature to do with the way we parent our children? Sometimes we're like those early scientists. We not only close our minds to how the balance principle works in nature and involuntarily in our bodies, we extend our denials to the natural mechanisms that provide for "gate valve" regulation and balance in our parenting lives. When principles supporting our *beliefs* about parenting are undeniable, we find adaption quite effortless and we learn and grow as more effective parents. However, when our beliefs are refutable (in error), the balancing force too often promotes a denial of truth, leading to stagnation and frustration.

The scientists who denied the outcome of Galileo's experiment were not refuting the evidence merely for the sake of "natural balance," as we think of it. They denied it because the results didn't match their *beliefs*. Nevertheless, nature's *truth* doesn't need our belief to make it factual. Truth is truth. Beliefs are always our choice. We can choose to align them with natural laws to help us maintain natural balance, or choose not to do so.

Balance and adaptability are clearly evident and essential in biology, physics, psychology, sociology, spirituality, and yes, even in the lighter side of our lives—sports, hobbies, and other interests. The natural *effects* of the balance principle can't be denied; however, they can arguably be adaptive or maladaptive. It's our job as parents to learn how to use the adaptive effects.

You Better Not or I'll Spank You

Let's think about how this principle could be influencing our beliefs about parenting. For example, we've heard people declare, "My parents spanked me, and I'm certainly not a child abuser." We assume, when we hear this, that spanking works and is effective as a disciplinary tool. There's another principle at work here that's subordinate to the principle of balance. It's the principle called "pain aversion," and it, indeed, tends to stop an unwanted behavior. Most of us want to avoid pain of any kind, as do our kids. This desire to avoid pain can be adaptive. In a natural setting, pain is typically higher up on the ladder of consequences. It serves as a warning, after other less pressing signs have been avoided. "Don't touch the hot stove! You'll burn yourself!" "If you run a red light, you might cause a car crash!" "Keep smoking and you might get lung cancer!" In these and other cases, the result of an event or choice can be immediately painful. Such cases generally involve high risk events, like heart failure, burns, broken bones, the loss of a loved one, and the like.

Spanking an unruly child typically stops an unwanted behavior immediately, because of the pain aversion principle. However, it can also be the catalyst for destructive and unbalanced emotions, such as anger, resentment, hostility, low self-worth, toxic guilt, and other negatives. Other empirical evidence suggests that spanking our children—as a means to seek obedience, impose discipline or teach respect—is clearly an *ineffective* way to guide them toward making adaptive choices; that is, to become capable, autonomous, balanced, and healthy adults. The body of scientific research is unequivocal regarding corporal punishment and very consistently reveals lasting negative effects on our children. Yet, this remains a controversial topic and recent surveys show that two-thirds of Americans still approve of parents spanking their kids.

A Screwdriver For A Nail?

When a hammer works better to drive a nail into two boards than a screwdriver does, we use the hammer. We don't use the screwdriver for that particular task. We also don't label the screwdriver as a worthless tool. If we change the scenario and use the screwdriver to insert a screw into the two boards, it becomes more valuable than the hammer for the task. If we try to hammer a screw into the wood, we're likely to split the wood, bend the screw, or fail in our efforts altogether. Our parenting methods include both "hammers" and "screwdrivers." Which one we use for a particular episode in our child's upbringing will make a lasting and visible impact. Make wise choices based on clear evidence.

What if we become like one of those scholars of Galileo's time that tends to "hang on" to invalid principles or results, regardless of seeing or learning a better one? Unfortunately, our senseless or willful disregard for reality will surely take its toll in one way or the other. In clinical terms, this indicates we're likely to develop hostility, anxiety, stress, anger issues, or depression. None of these is good for us or our children. In practical, everyday terms, denial of truth is a defense against the unknown and can be a balancing mechanism that keeps us "safe" from our fears (typically, fear of the unknown), but stuck. We're stuck, because the only way we can attempt to defend ourselves from the forces of fear and worry is to continue to depend on denial. To deny or avoid the unknown, we do what we know, even if it's invalid. If we know a better way that actually accomplishes our parenting goals and we use it, the fear subsides and adaptive balance is restored.

Why would we want to continue parenting in a way that doesn't work (like using spanking or shaming to speak for us), but expect that someday it *will* start to work (you know what they say about the definition of crazy)? If we continue to conduct ourselves in ways contrary to proven truths, to maintain our erroneous beliefs that spanking, screaming, shaming work, and to make choices that produce negative outcomes, we will be left with considerable discord and unhappiness within our family structures. If we violate, abuse or distort these natural principles of attachment, autonomy and adaptive balance, then we will lose the benefits they provide as the guiding and healing principles they were meant to be. Balance, in particular, keeps the family system in the optimal zone for teaching, learning, and loving.

When we watch our 9- to 14-month-old child work to place various-shaped blocks into their corresponding openings in a toy tower, we don't stop to think that many different learning factors are at work, including the process of repetition, the use of certain neuropsychological development skills, emotional regulation and even patience. If our child stubbornly attempts to place the triangle block into the round opening over and over again, his threshold of tolerance to frustration will soon be reached and we'll likely witness a temper tantrum. He becomes emotionally upset, hostile to the process of learning, and gives up trying to master the task. He may even throw the block across the room. Of course, all of these reactions are ineffective, and they soon exhaust supplies of important energy.

On the other hand, our flexibility in the use of trial and error and quickly finding a successful approach is reinforcing and produces adaptive balance. With this newfound balance, our children tend to learn more efficiently and develop better emotional control. The principle of flexibility is one of the necessary subsets of the balance principle.

Linking together all of the superordinate and subordinate principles of nature are, of course, way outside the scope of this book. But, we can start to see how using this conceptual model of primary and less primary principles to challenge our personal parenting principles will help us remain true to our power. Just like the lighthouse, we can shine our light. We can remain faithful to who we are. The acceptance of attachment, autonomy (independence; self-rule) and balance, as three viable principles, will help us relax in the comfort of our strength and stability as effective parents.

The principle of balance is necessary for peace, harmony and efficient learning in our family life. The methods of discipline we choose to utilize as parents should be effective in helping our children with their attachment, autonomy and balance.

Chapter 4
Bipolarity Principle

Reverse every natural instinct and do the opposite of what you are inclined to do, and you will probably come very close to having a perfect golf swing.
~Ben Hogan

For every action there is an equal and opposite government program.
~Bob Wells

THE BIPOLARITY PRINCIPLE is a more formal term for the "Opposites Principle." A philosopher by the name of Wittgenstein was the first to espouse the formal "bipolarity principle," which states that every proposition must be capable of being both true and false, or that there are always at least two options to every problem.

Bipolar simply means there are two poles. It assumes a scale, of sorts, between the two poles. For example, there is the North Pole and the South Pole. Or, there is hot and cold; big and little; tall and short, light and dark, and so forth. The extremes are the poles, but there is a gradient of these extremes in between the two poles.

Most of us will hear "bipolarity principle" and immediately think of bipolar disorder, a mental illness. We even use this term in popular western culture to describe anyone who displays a quick change in mood from seemingly happy to sad or irritable. Some of our older kids use this term in their speech. "Watch out! Mom's going bipolar again." Or, "Don't ask Dad, whatever you do! He's having one of his bipolar days."

Let's think broader about this interesting principle of nature. An understanding of its upside and its downside will prove useful in raising our children as power parents. As our children develop, they tend to define everything in their world in the concrete extremes of the bipolarity principle. That is, they view events or situations or dialogue as helpful or harmful; trustworthy or untrustworthy; good or bad; right or wrong; and yes or no. It's hard for them to make sense of "maybe" or "sometimes" or "on occasion." The middle is foggy or gray for them. Considering all the options in the middle takes some coordinated abstract thinking that will emerge later on, as they mature. The concrete is very useful and timely in this early stage of their development, however, and through their adolescence this kind of thinking represents the "ideal." Without an adequate number of difficult experiences grappling with the murky middle, they tend to be idealistic in their view of just about everything. As we did!

As we focus on the upside of this principle, our aim is to explore how polar opposites are related to two particular areas of our life—the emotional and the more practical. Let's take emotional distress as our first area. When we're feeling anxious (nervous, scared, apprehensive); we usually experience a few physical symptoms. Our central nervous system is activated and our heart may beat faster and pound in our chest, we may feel "flush" and sweaty, and we may breathe faster or find difficulty in breathing at all. If our anxiety escalates to an incapacitating level, we're likely to have what is called a *panic attack*.

Which comes first, the emotional experience or the physical symptoms? While this is an interesting question to contemplate, it's one that's not very practical for our purpose. Rather, we should focus on understanding some of the other factors involved in this biological and psychological phenomenon that we've all experienced many times to one degree or another. One area of interest that's related to the bipolarity principle is a built-in subset principle called *mutual exclusivity*. If we're tall, we can't be short. If we're behaving rudely, we can't be respectful simultaneously. If we're worried about something, we can't experience peace of mind. If our muscles are tense, they can't also be relaxed. So far, this is easy to understand. Now, let's think about something a little deeper. If we believe our thoughts—the intentional ones as well as the automatic ones (conscious and unconscious)—are occurring at the speed of light, then it's likely they're directly associated with our emotions and our bodily processes.

Our thoughts are our power. They're our engine. They pull the train of cars that carry our feelings, behaviors, and even a great share of our physiological reactions.

When the lighthouse was thinking scary thoughts about its treacherous environment, it experienced distress in the form of sadness, worry, self-doubt, and even guilt. The seagull guided its thinking back to the "positive opposite," and it started to experience excitement, strength, power, and clarity of purpose. There's a sense of real peace and calm that follows this kind of thinking. If we think scary thoughts, we experience scary feelings. Our behavior generally involves such things as avoidance (i.e., hiding, denying, and running), developing stress responses that are harmful to our body (i.e., over drinking, "road rage," speeding heart rate, chronic headaches, indigestion) and relinquishing our natural power.

There is a time to think, feel, and act scared. It's an automatic survival principle that can keep us alive in an emergency. The problem is when we start to generalize this automatic principle to our beliefs (thoughts) that are erroneous and not real emergencies. This can be one of the downsides. But, as long as we understand this principle with its subset principles, we can formulate a healthier relaxation response.

If we consciously invoke the most peaceful images or scenes imaginable, we will experience a relaxing of our emotions and our body. Our breathing will become regulated and our blood will become better oxygenated. Because our muscles will now be relaxed, our arteries, veins, and capillaries will be less constricted. As a result, our blood pressure will go down and so will our anxiety. Whenever we feel our muscles becoming tense, we should think relaxing thoughts. We can't be tense and relaxed at the same time. The two physical indicators are mutually exclusive of each other. They are bipolar elements.

What's this got to do with our parenting methods? It's intricately involved with the second practical use of the bipolarity principle and the management of our children's behavior. At times, we focus on their every little unwanted behavior. We know by now that if that's what we're thinking about, there's no way we'll experience happy and regulated emotions ourselves. Our stress will quickly rise to the "nosebleed level." Instead of focusing on the negative or disruptive behavior, we should focus on the most critical principles of healthy development—on creating balance and on using the positive opposite of the exhibited behavior. In so doing, we'll soon connect these principles with behavior management

Here's an example of how this works. Let's use the common unwanted behavior of our children speaking too loudly (yelling or screaming) in the house. We can talk with them about this until we're "blue in the face." If talking doesn't work, we can even try punishing this unwanted behavior away by spanking, removing privileges, or sending them to their rooms. We've already discussed why this doesn't work and the potential repercussions. The most successful plan is to reward the positive opposite. In this case, the preferred behavior (the positive opposite) is speaking quietly or in a normal tone of voice. If we're speaking quietly, we can't be speaking loudly. We can make speaking quietly worth our children's while with the rewards of compliments, hugs, pats on the head or shoulder, additional game or television time or even ice cream on occasion. Soon speaking quietly while in the house will become a habit that doesn't need rewarding.

Try this simple exercise. Read the description of this visual image first and then follow the directions. With your eyes closed, envision a huge, pink elephant with purple polka dots. Keep silently repeating to yourself, "Don't think about this huge pink elephant with purple polka dots. Don't think about this huge pink elephant with purple polka dots. Don't think about this huge pink elephant with purple polka dots." After about 60 seconds of following this protocol, open your eyes.

What image did you have in your mind's eye as you faithfully thought about not thinking about the elephant? That's right, the pink elephant with purple polka dots! We can only generate a visual image of our current thoughts. If, however, we substitute that thought with another thought that isn't related or associated with the elephant, we're able to accomplish not thinking about or envisioning the elephant. This is the way our brain works on positive feedback. It's related to the bipolarity principle and the subset of mutual exclusivity.

Not many of us ever give much thought about the polar opposites of "pessimism and optimism" as personality characteristics. As autonomous beings, with our sovereign power to choose, we will ultimately exercise our right of free choice each time we're confronted with a life event. The meaning we give this event will be more in the direction of one pole than the other. As we establish a trend toward one pole over the other, we will form a characteristic that becomes more pervasive over time. Our supreme power has its birth in the intentional way we choose to think about everything.

If our view is that pessimism is a limiting and negative force and that it will not likely serve us well; we can make a conscious decision to focus on its positive opposite. If we optimistically work toward viewing our outcomes as winners, our mind is prepped for creative solutions. Creative solutions and calamitous failures are mutually exclusive. Our power is in our choices, one-by-one. Sound thinking gives birth to correct and adaptive principles. If we practice these ourselves, we will habitually use the principles in the way we raise our children. We will teach them the fundamentals of the bipolarity principle vicariously ... that there are always, at the very least, two choices for every proposition or problem that comes up throughout every day of our life.

As parents, we can make a habit of choosing the positive opposite.

Chapter 5
Mutuality Principle

The community stagnates without the impulse of the individual. The impulse dies away without the sympathy of the community. ~William James, 1880

Interdependence is and ought to be as much the ideal of man as self-sufficiency. Man is a social being. Without interrelation with society he cannot realize his oneness with the universe or suppress his egotism. His social interdependence enables him to test his faith and to prove himself on the touchstone of reality. ~Mahatma Gandhi, 1929

LET'S REVIEW FOR just a moment. A strong and secure attachment is our necessary and first principle. It promotes a healthy sense of exploration and autonomy. Balance is critical in sustaining autonomy and attachment. Bipolarity or the "opposites" principle helps us understand the larger world of extremes and the middle gradient. With the help of balance, this bipolar principle brings to life, in very practical ways, the central importance in our autonomy (sovereign right to choose). As we help our children achieve skills with these core principles, in the context of our healthy family, we are creating a safe laboratory for them to experiment with the mutuality principle.

The mutuality principle assumes interdependency between at least two parties. It requires a reciprocal interconnectedness and responsibility *to* (not for) the other and sharing a common set of principles *with* the other. Being independent (developing and claiming autonomy) is a necessary first step, but it's not sufficient. When we're able to stand alone and commit to our own true identity, we're in a very good position to choose to connect to others with commitment. It also stands to reason that others—especially our children—will have a much better chance of knowing we're committing to them.

Independence ... The Grandchild Of Interdependence

Their "I can do it by myself" evolves into "I can now do for others." Many tribal cultures view independence as the grandchild of interdependence. Isn't that a nice metaphor? It suggests a trans-generational development component to family. All healthy and, therefore, sustainable interconnections are firmly based on the mutuality principle. It requires cooperation and doing things for the others in our family, work and social environments.

The Golden Rule

Who hasn't heard of the Golden Rule? This may be the very essence of the mutuality principle. In Matthew 7:12, Jesus said, "Do to others whatever you would like them to do to you. This is the essence of all that is taught in the law and the prophets." (NLT)

If we parents made this a central principle of relationships within our homes, what would be the effect on our world? This is a principle with unlimited power. It belongs, front and center, in our families. It's a law of nature, and it guides our choices in relating to each other. The effectiveness of our co-existing with each other and becoming more than a group of individuals depends on this guiding principle. Cooperation, compliance, and teamwork are possible, because of interdependence and doing for the other. In other words, "I will be responsible for myself, *and* I will be responsive to others."

There is definitely self-interest in the midst of the Golden Rule. "I will treat you the way I want to be treated." Within true mutuality or interdependency, there's an interesting relationship that exists between self-interest and other-interest, and a definite reciprocity. That is, "I will treat you the way I want to be treated, and you will treat me the way you would like to be treated." This method of relating suggests that mutuality requires a "responsibility for" and a "responsibility to." Notice the positive nature of this kind of action-oriented principle.

There are other principled teachings that emphasize the negative; such as, "Don't treat others the way you don't want to be treated." We avoid treating others badly, because we don't want to be treated badly. The result is generally good, in that we don't mistreat others, but look how powerful the Golden Rule is when stated in the active-positive. "*Purposely* go treat others just like you want to be treated." That makes this a very special principle that defines true mutuality and reinforces a proactive code of kindness.

This principle of mutuality requires autonomy with the addition of reciprocal connectedness. It means we need to be responsible for meeting our own needs, but we can't do this at anyone else's expense. Our responsibility to others doesn't allow it. We must ensure that our right to do for ourselves is extended to others so they can do for themselves. That way, there's a shared investment in both of our outcomes. If both our needs aren't met, then at least one of us loses his/her sovereign power. If this happens, then the relationship loses. There's no mutuality.

Manipulate with Integrity?

A mature form of manipulation can be included under this mutuality principle. In other words, there's a way to "manipulate with integrity." What? I know, that just doesn't sound right. But, if we can find creative ways to get our needs met, while we avoid doing so at the expense of others, then we've done so with integrity. Integrity, as used in this context, means to integrate pieces into a whole. Integrate these core principles into a meaningful self and we'll be able to "do for our self" as we "do for others."

It seems that all ethical standards in human activities are derived from the mutuality principle. The goodness in our world seems to be reflected by interdependency. There are all kinds of relationships, but arguably one of the most special is with our children. The mutuality principle requires that we do for our self *and* we do for our children. It also demands that we teach our children how to do for themselves and then do for others.

The Safe Laboratory

The family is the laboratory for developing this special relationship that's based on mutuality. It's the classroom for learning and incorporating these principles. It's not only a healthy way to live our lives; it also feels fair and balanced. There's something natural about living this way. It's reinforcing; therefore, it tends to make us want to play by these fair and natural laws. It helps us to see that the benefits of remaining connected far out-weigh the benefits of living alone. In other words, we and our children are motivated to cooperate with each other so we can continue to enjoy our mutual benefits.

The way we put this principle to work in our children's world starts with our responsibility to emotionally bond with them at birth. Through this seemingly selfish act of emotionally connecting to part of our self, we encourage an attachment from each child. Our children's attachments also seem purely based on self-interest, but it's their way of surviving. It also encourages their autonomy in the context of a mutual connection; hence, the wonderful metaphor of "independence is the grandchild of interdependence." We become more aware of their need to emotionally connect to us as we see their attempts to gain our attention and approval.

Love, Love, Love

Finally, and most importantly, it's because of the mutuality principle that we're able to develop the most powerful force known to us all—LOVE! This universal force is arguably the most supreme of all principles. It's so supreme that we typically just assume it's inextricably linked to all that's good, including our family relationships.

The word "love" has many different meanings to us. Unfortunately, in the English language, we're rather limited to the attaching of adjectives to describe these differences. Love is a concept that seems to be developmental. For example, some types of love appear to be subordinate to the greater love of charity and sacrifice. This kind of love, as C. S. Lewis states in his book, *The Four Loves*, is the kind of caring that emerges regardless of the circumstances. Lewis believed that this ultimate sacrificial love could not exist without the other subordinate kinds of love (affection, friendship, romantic, etc.).

Principled Parenting

Because we, as parents, can choose to live principally loving, caring and sacrificial lives, our children will not only feel connected to us, but will also be able to do the same. The family is such a wonderful primary and essential system for humanity. Its natural principles are equally elegant and awesome. Yet, when these principles aren't followed or when they're distorted, some of history's greatest atrocities have occurred. Every new generation depends on the family and, more specifically, on parents to play by the rules and get it right.

Our increased anxiety, depression, mean-spirited behavior, difficulty with education, apathy, and any of the other declines and problems for which we have opinions is directly related to the erosion or distortion of principled parenting.

It is exceedingly important for us to practice the mutuality principle. We must become an expert at doing for ourselves so that we can do for others. We must model this healthy principle for our children in everything we do, and then hold them accountable to this same principle of mutuality. If we are successful, they will likely live connected and enriched lives and pass it along to their children. Emulation is the highest form of flattery.

Chapter 6
Reinforcement Principle

The consequences of an act affect the probability of its occurring again.
~B.F. Skinner

EVERYTHING WE LEARN, from conception to death, requires use of the reinforcement principle. If we're constructing the foundation for a residential or commercial building, we use steel to reinforce the concrete slab. The steel strengthens the foundation. If we're learning a new set of skills at work, we must reinforce or strengthen them with a new set of behaviors. To that end, the reinforcement principle is natural and intuitive to us all.

Everything that's predictable has happened many times before. Predictable occurrences and their associations are reinforced each time they take place. When predictable things happen in our lives, we develop trust in them. Eventually, we take this principle for granted because of its regularity; but we don't stop to think that, without it, everything in our experience is turned upside down.

Understanding the reinforcement principle and its relationship with each of the other guiding principles increases our power. Just as reinforcement is powerful, so is its *bipolar opposite*—punishment. We use the term bipolar opposite only because one procedure *in*creases a behavior and the other *de*creases a behavior. But, both reinforcement and punishment are procedures that are either logically or naturally applied to a chosen act. Both bring consequences.

Strengthen Or Extinguish

A *reinforcer* is anything we apply to a behavior that increases the likelihood of that behavior happening again in the future. A *punisher* is anything we apply to a behavior that decreases the likelihood of that behavior occurring again in the future.

Our beliefs about these powerful consequences may actually be wrong. If they're erroneous, then our point of view needs to be realigned to match the natural principles. For example, most of us automatically believe that spanking a disobedient child is punishment. Spanking may, in fact, be a punisher; but, it may also be a reinforcer. The only way to know for sure is to assess whether the unwanted behavior of the child increases (reinforcer) or decreases (punisher) in the future.

Learn Your ABCs

Professionals in behavior like to think of them as having three parts and refer to them as the ABCs: the Antecedent, the Behavior, and the Consequence. The antecedent is what happens before the behavior. The consequence is what happens after the behavior.

Let's examine the following scenario. Eight-year-old Sammy is playing a video game in his room and his dad calls up the stairs, "It's time to turn off that game and go take your shower, son." (Antecedent.) "In a minute, Dad. I have to finish this game first." (Behavior-avoidance.)

"Turn it off and go take your shower. Immediately!" (Consequence.) Sammy continues to play his game. Ten minutes later, his dad shouts, "Sammy, if you're not in that shower in ten seconds flat, I'll bust your bottom!" (Second consequence.)

"Okay, okay, Dad. I'm going," (Second behavioral response) Sammy stands up, but continues to play. (Avoidance.) Approximately five minutes later, Sammy's dad rushes up the stairs and into Sammy's room. "Are you looking for a spanking? Get into that shower, now! That's an order!" (Third consequence.) Sammy turns off the game and dashes into the bathroom. (Third behavioral response: compliance.)

Was the consequence the father applied the first and second time reinforcement or punishment? The consequences applied were reinforcements, because the procedure of shouting out orders and threats actually *in*creased the probability of avoidant behavior on Sammy's part! We might say that the third consequence of Dad's marching into the room and threatening to spank Sammy was a punishment, because it *de*creased the likelihood of more avoidant behavior on Sammy's part.

Who Is Conditioning Who?

However, let's examine a shift in our rationalization. Could it be that what just occurred in this scenario was Sammy conditioning his dad to lose his temper and become more threatening, while all along he was avoiding an unattractive choice? The ultimate reinforcement of Dad's permissive behavior is when Sammy *chose* to comply on the third consequence and, thereby, removes Dad's frustration and allows him to feel successful.

There was reinforcement for Dad's permissive behavior and escalated frustration, and there was reinforcement for Sammy's avoidant behavior. Sammy's choice to comply was reinforced only when the threat of pain from a spanking became greater than the pain of turning the game off to take an unwanted shower. Consequently, this behavioral cycle continues.

The reason we need to make this shift in our point of view (paradigm), as a power parent eager to establish a healthy family environment, is that reinforcement and punishment are very powerful, and there are natural and intuitive ways for us to maximize their effectiveness. We need to utilize them purposefully and precisely. Spanking isn't always a punisher, and when it is, it's usually effective in stopping a behavior each time it's utilized. The actual threat or execution of this painful stimulus is reinforced each time Sammy refuses to comply, until he's made to comply, by either an external threat or aversive stimulus. Spanking also reinforces (strengthens) anxiety, anger, guilt and resentment.

Another important factor at work within the reinforcement principle is "valence." Valence is a psychological value placed on anything. It's typically viewed as positive or negative, or in psychological terms, as pleasurable and aversive. Therefore, the valence attributed to a consequence can be positive, desirable, pleasurable, or good; or, it can be negative, undesirable, aversive, or bad. Reinforcement occurs only when the consequence is a reinforcer (increases the probability of the desired behavior to reoccur). Typically, this will involve something pleasurable.

Sibling Squabble

Let's consider a situation where Suzie's sister Patty takes her iPod. (Antecedent.) Suzie yanks on Patty's hair and tells her, "I'll only let go when you give me back my iPod!"

Patty hands over the iPod (Behavior) and Suzie stops pulling her hair (Consequence: negative reinforcement.). Subtracting the pain is reinforcing the behavior (returning the iPod). This is an example of negative reinforcement. The removal of the undesirable consequence (pulled hair equals pain) reinforced the behavior of returning the iPod. It is negative reinforcement, because the objectionable stimulus was subtracted or removed. Torment of any kind is considered a negative reinforcer only if the subject being under attack gives verifiable information and the tormenter stops the unwanted behavior after receiving the information.

The same is true for punishment. It typically involves something undesirable. But, what if Suzie refuses to obey her parents? For example, they reasonably ask her to meet them at the front of the school building at 4:00 p.m., soon after the school day ends. They arrive at the scheduled time and Suzie isn't there waiting. They wait for ten minutes and then set out to find her. Suzie had decided she wanted to watch the girls' volley ball game, instead of complying with her parents' request. As a result, Suzie and her parents were late for her important appointment with the orthodontist.

For the sake of this example, let's assume Suzie's parents have a simple behavior management plan for her. This plan honors Suzie's choice, while at the same time incorporating built-in consequences intended to punish noncompliance while also reinforcing compliance. Her father reminds her that because of her noncompliance, she's now on "shut-down" and has no access to her privileges until she chooses to cooperate and pay off her debt. She owes her parents an E.B.T. (Early Bed Time), which involves going to bed one hour earlier than her established bedtime. This is the only way Suzie can earn back her privileges.

But, there's a problem. "I can't do that tonight!" Suzie wails. "I have to go to Amy's birthday party. I can't not show up. She's my best friend!"

Her parents shrug. "Sorry, Suzie, you know the rules. Your earlier personal choice placed you on shut-down, and you don't have access to your privileges until you pay back the E.B.T."

Negative Punishment?

Now here's where the negative punishment comes in. Suzie enjoys her privileges (desirable-positive valence), and yet she's lost them by her previous choice (undesirable-negative valence; negative punishment). When she chooses to pay back the E.B.T. (compliant and cooperative behavior), she regains her privileges (positive reinforcement). Negative punishment is when we remove or subtract something that has positive/desirable valence, and the previous unwanted behavior (noncompliance) is decreased.

In this example, Suzie's parents have essentially used a "double-barreled shotgun" to blast the target (noncompliant behavior). They have used negative punishment by removing Suzie's desirables (privileges), and positively reinforced compliant behavior by adding desirables (access to privileges) after a choice of cooperation. Suzie chose to break the rule and she lost the privilege to attend her best friend's birthday party.

When we think about the reinforcement principle, we're typically describing how nature and other people are responding to our actions, especially our children. Keep in mind that we're also reinforcing ourselves. Self-reinforcement is an important aspect of the reinforcement principle. It can either facilitate or inhibit adaptation.

Superheroes!

Years ago, I was involved in the treatment of a young man from the time he was in elementary school through high school. He was emotionally immature and, consequently, had difficulty with age-appropriate social skills. At age sixteen, he continued to have rich fantasies about being a "Superhero." He collected little trinkets related to Batman, Iron Man, and other well-known characters. You can imagine how he was treated by his peers as he talked about and showed them his collectables. He was made fun of, called cruel names, and humiliated (punishment).

Why didn't he stop this childish behavior? Because the "self-reinforcement" he delivered continued to be more powerful than the so-called "punishment" his peers delivered. In other words, the positive value attributed to his wish-fulfillment (viewing himself as a Superhero) was a strong "self-reinforcer," and the negative value attributed to his humiliating treatment by peers (punisher) was not as strong as the self-reinforcer. It meant more to him to play this childlike fantasy role than it did for him to try to fit in with his peers, perhaps because he didn't believe it was possible for him to ever "fit in." Self-reinforcement can be adaptive or maladaptive.

What if this young man had been able to learn the specific skills that epitomize the positive aspects of a Superhero's lifestyle? You know, like being kind and helpful to others or living a principled life of treating others the way he wanted to be treated. That's, of course, the psychological theme of Superheroes. They are somehow unable to live in a "grand" way *until* they are magically transformed with their mask, special uniform, and tools of the "Superhero" trade. Then, and only then, do they have the special powers to be special to others.

When we self-reinforce the behaviors of ourselves and our children, associated with this kind of principled living, we'll likely find that nature and most of those in our environment will also reinforce our choices. This becomes adaptive and is naturally associated with our emotional maturity. Then, there's no need for the fantasy symbols of a mask or uniform or magic wands. Adaptive self-reinforcement is a necessary ingredient in the recipe for self-control.

If we want to become power parents, we must pay closer attention to what strengthens healthy and adaptive behaviors and to what tends to extinguish unhealthy and maladaptive behaviors. We must be consistent in practicing what we learn. If we do, we'll soon become an expert in the behavior management of our children. The reinforcement principle can be our best friend.

Premack Principle

A subset of the reinforcement principle is the Premack principle. Dr. David Premack, a professor of psychology, conducted monkey research in the late 1950s that led to scientifically describing this powerful behavioral principle, which states, in behavioral terms, that any high-frequency activity (eating ice cream) can be used to reinforce any low-frequency activity (eating spinach). This is fondly known as Grandma's Rule.

As good behavior managers, we've learned now that we don't modify behavior; rather, we modify the environment (antecedents and consequences). Then, the behaviors of our children change. Notice how this point of view (principle) is consistent with the earlier discussed principles of autonomy, balance, bipolarity, mutuality, and reinforcement, all of which support this notion of managing the environment and extending the natural right of choice to our children for their own behavior.

High-frequency activities are usually high-interest activities that have a very positive valence or value. With our children, these activities could include playing video games, watching TV, participating in sports or cheerleading, attending outings with their friends, driving the family car, or having a friend over to play. We can fill in the rest of the list for our specific children. Low-frequency activities, on the contrary, are usually low-interest activities that carry a negative valence. For our children, this might include doing homework, taking out the garbage, washing supper dishes, cleaning their room, brushing their teeth twice a day, taking a shower or bath before bedtime, practicing the piano. Again, this list will vary.

As power parents, we should strive to use high-frequency activities as an incentive for completing low-frequency activities. If the value our children place on a high-frequency activity (eating ice cream) is strong enough, it will reinforce the completion of a lower-frequency activity (eating spinach).

Popeye The What?
When these natural principles are distorted and turned "upside-down," I am reminded of one of my favorite childhood Sunday cartoons, "Popeye the Sailor Man." Popeye's best friend, Wimpy, was his polar opposite. Basically, Popeye lived his life based on personal integrity, bravery, selflessness, and purposeful ambition. Wimpy, on the other hand, epitomized laziness, cowardice, and selfishness. So much so that his life's mantra was, "I'll gladly pay you Tuesday for a hamburger today."[1]

Why is it that we can quickly understand the absurdity of such behavior in a cartoon character, yet have difficulty recognizing the absurdity in the behavior of our children or ourselves? It may have something to do with the comic relief that accompanies the recognition of us in the cartoon character. The seriousness of the consequences of distorting these principles in our own lives and the lack of perceived options makes us want to run and hide.

PICNIC
Information Technology professionals have a saying that is used after troubleshooting employees' computer and telecommunication systems and not finding a problem with the hardware or the software. PICNIC! "Problem In Chair Not In Computer." This book is not about blaming parents, or children for that matter. It's about taking responsibility, learning skills that work, and teaching the skills to our

children. After evaluating a child and his parent's discipline methods and style I will sometimes write in the chart "PICNIC" (Problem In Caregiver Not In Child) to remind me to focus on effective management skills for the parents.

As power parents, we can become more perceptive and exceptional managers within our family unit when we utilize consistent and unforgiving principles that are recognized and respected by every member. Grandma's Rule can help us accomplish this goal and provide our children with increasing autonomy (self-reliance) and balance.

Chapter 7
Parsimony Principle

Keep it simple stupid. ~Kelly Johnson

KISS

KELLY JOHNSON WAS the lead engineer at the "Lockheed Skunk Works" that created such notable spy planes as the U-2 and the SR-71. Reportedly, he gave his team the challenge to design an aircraft that could be repaired by average mechanics with only a handful of tools while in the field and under combat conditions. Johnson's KISS Principle (keep it simple stupid) referred to the fact that, until that time, most military aircraft were so complex in structure they required a great deal of sophistication to fix. There was an urgent need to keep future designs simple. Today, the KISS principle is used in every kind of business design, in law, sports and even fashion.

KISS is the opposite of information overload. It involves the uncluttering of our thoughts and communication. It reduces complexity. It reminds us to "keep it short and to the point."

The word "parsimony" is related to the word "simple." It's usually defined as frugality or stinginess; however, in using the term

"Parsimony Principle" as one our seven guiding principles for creating a happy family, we're referring to KISS simplicity. The simplest explanations and directions, when communicating with our children, is usually the best. It tends to emphasize "common sense" and the straightforwardness found in natural laws.

Who's Razor?

The parsimony principle, as a philosophical tool, was further developed in the fifteenth century by an English Franciscan friar by the name of William of Ockham. He stated, "Entities must not be multiplied beyond necessity." In other words, the simplest answer to any problem is usually the correct answer. This principle became known as "Ockham's razor," and was used as a rule of thumb to guide scientists in the development of theories. The razor refers to their need to shave away everything that wasn't needed, so they could get to the least complicated explanation.

The word "simplicity" has a soothing sound to it. But rearing children, while working in a complicated and fast-paced world and living frenetic lives to stay in the game, is anything but easy. We have a challenge similar to that of Kelly Johnson and his design team. We need to create the most functionally simple plan for managing our modern families, and the models we build must not only be uncomplicated and natural, they must be portable. That is to say, we must be able to pick them up, take them with us, and apply them anywhere and at any time our children are with us—at the ballgame, Grandma's house, in the movie theater, at the grocery store. Wherever. That's the beauty in reducing all of the complex factors of parenting down to a few basic guiding principles. For instance, "Remember to say please and thank you." "Don't touch things belonging to someone else, without having permission." "Don't take anything that doesn't belong to you, tell lies, or be mean-spirited."

Natural principles are intuitive and, therefore, self-evident. They're based on common sense. They shave away the unnecessary complexities and assumptions that too often generate and sustain stress—stress that's associated with our sense of helplessness and hopelessness and, yes, even our sense of incompetence. Chronic stress distorts our values and all that we know to be true, while wreaking havoc on our physical and spiritual selves.

We all have the ability to develop an effective plan for accomplishing our family goals. It just takes commitment and know-how, which we're in process of learning. Our job is to take our newfound knowledge, integrate it with our personal values and unique lifestyle, and make it work for us and our family, all the while remembering that the parsimony principle will be our greatest helper. KISS!

PART II
Putting the Principles to Work

Chapter 8
The Starting Line

OUR CHILDREN TEND to provide what we need the most as parents—abundant opportunities for practicing *patience*! That's why we need a parenting plan. Without one, even minor incidents can produce *im*patience, and impatience usually produces more complicated problems.

Throughout our lifetime, we've been told by our own parents, grandparents, school teachers and even bosses that "practice makes perfect," especially when applied to skills we must acquire to become good or, hopefully, expert in any given undertaking. That's how we became a good enough musician to join the high school band or orchestra, to make the varsity basketball team, to earn a place on the college debate team, to be hired as a manager in our company, and so forth. Most of the time, practice either perfects our adaptive skills or, conversely, our maladaptive skills, depending on how and what we practice. Either way, our endeavors require patience. Lots of it.

Right now, at this moment, we can choose to develop patience when it comes to changing a few of our ineffective parenting methods for new, more successful ones. We'll eventually get it right, but it will take some time. The positive outcome, however, will fill us with pride, increased joy, and peace. We deserve it. Our family deserves it. The more patient we become, the easier it will be for us to choose to be a composed and powerful parent.

First, we must understand that our *thoughts are the regulators of our emotions.* Family living and parenting are emotionally charged endeavors. We must learn to recognize when our various emotions are bubbling to the surface at a moment of crisis and choose to act patiently and rationally before taking action or saying something that will wound rather than improve. In time, our ability to be patient will become habitual and will serve us well. Our positive attitudes, fueled by our optimistic thoughts and beliefs, will dictate how we live our lives, and we won't be ruled by our spur-of-the-moment emotional reactions.

Shake it Off and Step Up

This particular story demonstrates how important our attitude is in the face of any challenge. A farmer had a geriatric mule that fell into an old water well. The farmer heard the mule making a ruckus in the well and knew he needed to do something about the situation. After giving it careful thought, he decided that neither the mule nor the well was worth saving. He called his neighbors and friends and asked if they would help him haul enough dirt to bury the old mule in the well and put him out of his misery.

As you can imagine, the old mule became even more distraught when he figured out their intentions. But, as the farmer and his friends tossed one shovelful of dirt after the other onto his back, it dawned on him that every time one landed on him, he should shake it off and step up! This he did, time after time. "Shake it off and step up. Shake it off and step up." He repeated the mantra to bolster his courage and determination. No matter how distressing the situation was, he fought his sense of panic and kept right on shaking off the dirt and stepping up on the growing pile under his hooves. It wasn't long before the old mule, battered and exhausted, stepped triumphantly over the wall of that well.

Isn't that the way life is for most of us? We feel that shovelfuls of adversities are being tossed at us nonstop. Parenthood is replete with difficulties. We don't have to give up and succumb to becoming a victim buried by a load of burdens that seem insurmountable. If we face them bravely and respond to them positively and refuse to give in to a sense of panic or bitterness or self-pity, they can either be overcome or minimized in importance. Every age of our children comes with its own problems, and we must practice patience as we learn how to deal with them.

Let's remember that our children face their own shovelfuls of challenges in school, at home, and in their social lives. They are bound to become as discouraged, angry, frustrated, impatient, or scared as we are, and reveal a host of other emotions as they try to "deal" with endless issues while making a place for themselves in their world of peers. As parents, we are their primary role models. If we allow our inappropriate emotions to clash with theirs, we can create even more chaos.

That's why our ability to practice patience is so critically important. Patience will allow us to remain hopeful, positive, creative, and eventually successful in our ability to handle each crisis. Like the old mule, we must "shake it off and step up" to parenting challenges, and in the process, teach our children to do the same with their own. Our attitude greatly affects the quality of our parenting and, ultimately, to the quality of our lives and theirs as we strive to build a happier family. Positive attitudes are contagious.

Become a Good Scientist

George Kelly, a psychologist and personality theorist in the 1950s and 1960s, believed we are our own "personal scientists" and that our responsibility is to be a good one.

Our family can be a safe and ideal laboratory for sharpening our scientific skills. A good scientist observes and tests and tries to control all variables, in order to either validate or invalidate theories and hunches. A good scientist hangs on to the valid and reliable results and lets go of the invalid results. They aren't useful, and further research will be less encumbered and more efficient without them. As parental "scientists" then, we must examine and test and use each of the seven guiding principles we've been discussing, throwing out some of our proven invalid methods as being no longer useful and focusing on formulating a more workable process that brings about the best results.

Scientists must be rational in their research efforts and use proven methods that will be acceptable to others in their field of endeavor. As personal scientists, we must also use rational methods in our relational roles as parents within our family structure. First, we must know our purpose. As the biological donors or adoptive parents, we're the dutiful caretakers. We "love" our children. This is certainly necessary, but, unfortunately, it's not sufficient. As parental scientists, we must know the rules and be purposeful and intentional. Parenting involves something more than merely loving. How have we chosen to parent our children? What are we trying to accomplish?

Here are a few ideas to consider:

- I want to ensure my children are as mentally and physically healthy as they can be and understand their rights to "life, liberty, and the pursuit of happiness."
- I want to be their teacher, their go-to-person, and the one who guides and helps them as they learn to do things by themselves.
- I want to provide the supportive framework and environment for this process to unfold.
- I want to be their untiring encourager.
- I want to provide the type of governing relationship that allows them to make choices that work for them, through their own experiences.
- I want to have a strong and mutually satisfying relationship with my children, even when they are adults, which will enable me to have a happy relationship with my grandchildren.

What a powerful way to connect two or three generations and plant the seeds of our influence on many generations to come!

Why clarify and formulate our parenting intentions in the manner of a personal scientist? Because our intentions involve our rights and also the rights of our children. These rights are not devised through random and coincidental events. What we may have wanted from our parents or grandparents and didn't receive doesn't have to affect what we choose to do now and in the future. By patiently practicing use of the seven principles for creating a happier family, we can produce different results. Our children will develop appropriate stronger attachments and "self-regulation." They will become self-managers who are well-connected. They will develop self-control and be happier individuals who are less hostile toward others. When they're taking personal responsibility for their actions and speech and practicing self-regulation, others will respect them and allow them to live their lives without interference.

Define Your Family Situation
In the traditional situation, a family would consist of two married heterosexual parents who are committed to working jointly towards the creation of a happy unit. In today's world, however, this situation may not always exist. The National Marriage Project at Rutgers University issued a report called *The State of Our Unions 2005*. It revealed that 8.1 percent of coupled households consist of unmarried heterosexual partners. It also reports that only 63 percent of American children grow up with both biological parents. This is the lowest figure in the Western world. There are other situations involving homosexual partners, single parents, blended families, foster families, and grandparents performing the parenting role. These factors may make some parenting responsibilities more difficult, but the personal responsibility of each caretaker adult and the governing principles remain the same.

To review something we've already discussed, at the very core of our caretaker responsibility is the need to "emotionally bond" with our children. This usually occurs at or around birth. If, for whatever reason, this is not accomplished, it needs to happen nonetheless. Accomplishment of this task allows our children to "attach" to us. This forms the relationship—the connection—that is the context for guiding them through the stages of childhood. It is also required for behavior management.

It takes two to have a connection or relationship. The only way this happens is to first do our part—bond with our children. Then they will do their part—attach to us. The bottom line? Before we can make use of the seven guiding principles to create a happier family, we must first define our family situation, and then access our thoughts, emotions, and behaviors that are necessary to ensure our children have a strong bond with us. If for some reason we are unable or incapable of doing this, our children will need others in their lives that can provide this essential connection for them. Our job is to make this happen.

The late Mother Teresa, well-known for her optimism and generous giving of love and service to the unfortunate in India, was reported to have had many visitors and letters with requests to help with her work. When asked what they could do to help, she reportedly said, (paraphrasing) "Go home and take care of your own responsibilities so that I won't have to." We mustn't miss the importance of this profound response. We should be such responsible and effective parents so that our children will do the same in their relationships, and then we will have considerably less need for the level and kind of charity provided by people like Mother Teresa.

An early healthy relationship with our children that provides for strong bonding and attaching sets the stage for all that will follow. It is the basis for successful guidance, external discipline, and behavioral management. It is at the core of "self-interest," which motivates our children to choose to comply and cooperate with us. We must make whatever time is necessary to nurture this connection throughout our children's lives.

Again, this begins in those first few weeks of life. When our children are infants, we must hold and caress them with all the tender and loving emotion we can muster. We must meet all their dependency needs, so they learn we are trustworthy and dependable. We need to smile as often as possible and find ways to invest other positive affection and physical time with them.

What comes next? None of us outgrows the need or desire to hear such things as, "You are one remarkable kid/person. I don't know what I'd do without you." "The world is a better place, because you're in it." "You are one of a kind. You can do and be whatever you choose. I'll support you all I can." "I'm so lucky to have you in my life." Our children will bask in the glow of such words and respond in positive ways. They'll want to live up to them. Our relationships with them will grow stronger and the responses we receive will definitely influence our daily behaviors and attitude. Regardless of our home family situation, purposeful, positive parental/caretaker behavior strengthens the connection to our children.

A great byproduct of choosing to live this way is that it inoculates both our children and us against the harmful effects of the stress we experience each day. It's the best medicine for the body, mind, and soul.

Fly the Family Airplane

When I was learning to fly airplanes, I had an instructor who had once flown bombers in Korea, and specifically, the B-52 in Vietnam. After he retired from the U.S. Air Force, he trained new U.S.A.F. pilots and civilian private pilots. Dale used to say, "Fly the airplane! No matter what happens, fly the plane." Although it seemed like a given, what he meant was that even if things weren't going the way they were supposed to go, the pilot needed to focus on flying the airplane and not become distracted.

In the middle of a family crisis, our number one task is to fly the airplane. That may not be natural for us. Everyone's emotions are going wild, fear and adrenaline are in no short supply, and, yet, someone needs to fly that plane if we are to return in one piece to our beloved *terra firma*. The natural laws of gravity and aerodynamics are at work when piloting a plane. Thrust, drag, lift, and the downward force of gravity are influencing the plane, even if the engine stops. We can land that plane without a working engine; but we must follow the predictable rules if we want to manage gravity in a controlled manner and land safely.

The pilot has to control the surface of the plane and its attitude, especially in a crisis. This takes planning and training. Most of the training focuses on staying clear of crises. Sometimes, however, the unintended happens and good training allows the pilot to follow the rules and remain focused on the job, flying the airplane. We parents are the pilots of our family plane. Regardless of the crisis of the moment, we need to fly the plane.

A particular story was frequently told around the local airports when I was flying planes as a private pilot. Older pilots enjoy their "hanger talk." It seems that a local instructor pilot and F.A.A.-designated examiner was in the right seat of a Cessna 152 next to a student pilot who was flying the aircraft. It was to be a normal day of flying, with the student doing some typical maneuvers in the local practice area: slow flight, steep turns, and stalls and falls. Without warning, the propeller and the front part of the Cessna engine went flying into the atmosphere. It was a major catastrophe! The instructor immediately took over the controls and methodically worked through the emergency landing checklist and landed the critically disabled plane in a nearby field. Both the instructor and the student pilot climbed out of the plane and walked to safety, albeit with wobbly knees and a metal taste in their mouths. Later, they were told that instructor pilots were being trained in a T-38 and T-37 from the nearby U.S. Air Force base. A T-38 had collided with them mid-air.

For a student pilot, hearing a story like this one could either bring comfort, knowing it was possible to steer a crippled plane to safety, or make him/her decide to end flying lessons forever. Each pilot would make a personal choice, depending upon how the story affected his/her emotions and thoughts.

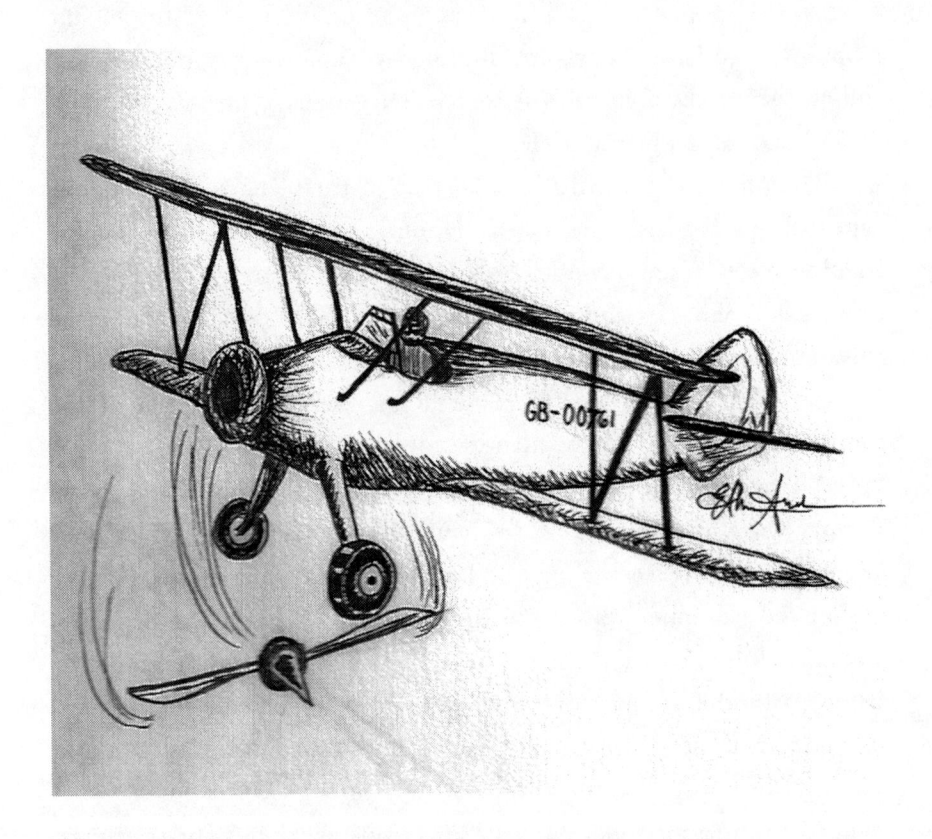

All human beings have a wide variety of emotions. They are natural components of our makeup. We will exhibit our emotions in one way or another on a daily basis. The challenge for us as parents is to regulate them with the skills and logical thinking of a well-trained pilot so that we can "fly the plane" to safety, regardless of the severity of the family crisis.

Most people are convinced that learning to fly an airplane is difficult (it isn't). Some are afraid to try and others jump at the opportunity. Life in general is like that. Some of our pre-teen and teenaged children are afraid to grow up and others can't wait for the next adventure that brings more independence. In either case, they need a great instructor(s) and lots of opportunities to practice and to learn from mistakes, as they develop the skills and self-confidence to fly solo.

After learning the basics of flying an airplane and then passing the solo flight around the airport several times, a student pilot must plan a cross-country flight and venture into unknown territory. A successful flight brings soaring self-confidence and the opportunity to prove proficiency by becoming a licensed pilot who can take on passengers. This won't happen, however, unless the check-ride is passed. An F.A.A. examiner takes the budding pilot through a long check-list of maneuvers which must be executed correctly, or no license is forthcoming. In everyday life, none of us have to pass a check-list before we take off on our own. And we certainly don't have to pass a test before we have children.

Flying solo as a licensed pilot can be likened to becoming totally independent and skillful in living our daily life. At some point, we graduate to flying with a copilot, and at times we fly as the copilot. We learn to work interdependently as part of a flight crew. We learn cooperation and trust and reliability. So it is in our family unit. We occasionally fly as a pilot, but more often as a copilot with our partner; we are committed in our relationship and conscientiously practice our parenting skills in all kinds of situations. The better prepared we are to manage any type of "in-flight" crisis, the more enjoyable the flight will be. It takes many skills and constant vigilance. We both become experts and know how to function in either of our roles so that, when called upon, we can step up and do what needs to be done. Usually, when we're comfortable and confident in our ability to work seamlessly as a crew member, we can take on passengers—our kids.

We start out by teaching them to be well informed passengers. We teach them everything we can about the rules and how the "plane" works. Before long, they're interested in learning how to take over the flight by themselves. This family plane is a wonderful vehicle for seeing and experiencing the world. We learn to plan well for all kinds of contingencies, but inevitably, there are some surprises with weather, changes with instructions from the air traffic controllers, and a need to divert to a new airport. We can't control all the variables, but we can be a well-trained and capable crew that is able to problem solve so that most flights are safe and successful ones.

Being Better Together
I don't intend this next statement to be a commentary on divorce; it's just an observation of what tends to keep us together. If we're steadfast in our efforts to be the best crew we can be, it isn't as likely that we'll be looking for others to fly the family plane. When we become seamless and everything seems right, we'll want to stick with our partner. And, please take note; it's never the right time to run out on our partner in the middle of a crisis. We must get back to safety and debrief and try to improve our communication and skills as quickly as possible. Our children's security and happiness depends on our ability to work out any glitches. However, even if we're divorced already, our other parental partner must still "fly the plane."

There are times we enjoy flying on our own. We need times like that to stay sharp and confident in our personal scientist skills and independence. But, we choose to keep flying together as copilots, because we have learned how to be interdependent. When we make our flight as parents work better if we're together, rather than on our own, there is clear reason to remain together.

Chapter 9
Power-Parent Skills

EXACTLY WHAT ARE the skills we need to become an effective power parent? Although there are likely many more, the following list is a starting point.

- Mindful Observation
- Accurate Assessment
- Rational Judgment and Perception
- Clear Communication
- Enthusiastic Experimentation
- Persistent Plan Preparation
- Diligent Implementation
- Resolute Re-evaluation
- Agreeable Adaptation
- Relaxation and Recreation

Mindful Observation
It takes considerable training to accurately observe what is going on around us in our homes, but it's a skill we can develop over time. It entails using all our senses. Our eyes, ears, and nose are all involved,

as are our senses of taste and touch, and when we use them consistently and wisely, they will serve us well in our parenting or co-parenting roles. It's possible, of course, for us to go through any day with a minimum level of sensory input and our evaluation of matters will still function, but we define this level as "just making it." This is how most of us function, until we become aware of what little effort we're putting into our parental responsibility and the consequences of our deficiencies.

How many times have we come home from our office or place of business, parked our car in the garage, seen the bicycle in the flowerbed or skateboard near the street and not wondered who they belonged to or why they were there? Or walked up the stairs to our bedroom to change clothes and stepped over the toys littering the steps rather than picking them up or immediately finding the owners and discussed the potential danger? Or noticed that the children were watching television or arguing in the family room over whose turn it was to use the Wii game, instead of doing their homework? How many times have we missed seeing the teary eyes of our wife or the deep scowl on the face of our husband or ignored the constant bickering of our children and remained mute? Our senses are usually turned "inward" on ourselves, and we have become habitually blind, deaf and mute to those who share our home environment.

To fully develop our senses for watchful awareness, we must consciously choose to live a different way. A more mature attentiveness and mindfulness allows us to place our experiences in an orderly form. It takes concerted effort, and by the end of a workday we're usually not in the mood to put forth much effort. We just want to relax in peace and quiet or have someone wait on us. Unfortunately, this is rarely possible when we decide to bring children into our world.

As the demands of parenting increase with the numbers and ages of our children, trying to live a rich and meaningful life becomes harder, especially when we have to juggle these demands with our increased work load and social responsibilities outside our home. We'll need skills that are consistent and come naturally to us, so we can conserve energy and make our input count in a positive way. It is possible to relax and enjoy peace and relative quiet at home if we have the understanding and cooperation of every member who respects the "space" of the others.

How do we do this? For starters, we can decide to spend a day using our listening, seeing, and touching senses at least twice as often as our speaking skill (two ears, eyes, and hands and only one mouth). We can purposefully and more keenly observe our children, spouse and environment. Then, at the end of the day, we can jot down a few of our discoveries. Some (most!) will likely surprise us, but they'll provide a better picture of the inadequate quality of our skill set and of how much we've been missing on an ordinary day.

Our closer observation brings a few questions to mind. How much has each of our children grown in size over the past six months? What new skills has each developed? Which ones need our input or instruction? Who needs a haircut? Who's ready to be taught how to ride a bicycle or drive a car? Whose manners need refining? Who helps with the preparation of supper or feeds the dog without being asked? Who remembers to carry her dirty dishes to the sink after eating? Who has a new hairstyle? Is Billy squinting as he reads and turning his head slightly to one side? Maybe he needs an eye exam for glasses. Who has a temper problem? Who whines when she communicates her needs or wants? Who is spending far too much time texting messages to friends? Who consistently lies when caught disobeying family rules ... and why?

Mindful observational skills are necessary for us as caring parents who want to accurately assess the behavior of our children, the level of their capabilities, their individual needs, their untiring effort or accomplishments, growth, participation in family activities and conversations and so forth.

Accurate Assessment

As we become skillful in using all our senses for mindful observation of our children, we have a great deal of good data to evaluate. Our goal is to close the gap between what we say we value and how we choose to conduct ourselves as parents to achieve these values. If we've just been on automatic pilot, not fully conscious of the behaviors of our children and why they are or aren't acceptable, or how far they've progressed in their development and age-appropriate achievements, then our parenting course is in error and in need of an adjustment.

After honing our skills of mindful observation, we'll be able to accurately appraise each situation and choose to get back on our chosen course—one that will take us to our preferred destination, which might include finding that peaceful oasis where we can refuel for the next day. Both skills require focus and time and resolve. Both are desirable, not only for our personal reasons, but because we care deeply about the quality of the daily lives of our children and their ability to enjoy each new challenge and accomplishment.

Discussing the quality of our personal skills with our partner is helpful, to see if we're on course together as we embark on self-improvement of our parenting methods.

Rational Judgment And Perception

Our brain, the generator of thoughts, is an amazing power plant and command center for all that transpires in our lives. It's been estimated that we have around 60,000 thoughts each day. There's no way to keep up with that many. Most are beneath the threshold of our awareness anyway. Some are automatic and reflexive. For example, at the end of the day, our brain releases hormones that allow us to go to sleep. We need sleep for all sorts of things to ensure we maintain our health. While we're asleep, we're unconscious, but we don't have to worry about several functions that keep us alive. The lower part of the brain (called the medulla oblongata ... you gotta to love these names) still regulates our heart rate, blood pressure, respiration, kidney functions, and so on. Failing to get enough sleep or sleeping at odd hours not only makes us bleary-eyed throughout the day—and perhaps a little crotchety with family members or those at work—it can also heighten our risk for a variety of major illnesses and decrease our ability to focus and remember. This is why we must carefully monitor how much sleep our children get at every age. In order to perform to the best of their ability at school, they need deep, dreaming sleep.

While we sleep, we dream. Dreaming is unconscious thought. Why do we dream and do our dreams serve any purpose? While researchers have worked on the answer to these questions and come up with many theories over the decades, no single consensus has materialized. For them and for us, dreams remain baffling. Nevertheless, some researchers suggest that dreaming is essential to our mental, emotional and physical well-being. The bottom line is that we have no control over when or how often we dream during our sleeping hours and no control over the content.

During our waking hours, however, we do have some control over the content of our thoughts. For instance, we can choose to think rationally (reasonably, realistically, logically) and hone our skills of observation and perception. Our thinking is our guidance system. Did you know that the same subatomic particles that form matter and energy in the rest of our universe are also found in our thoughts? If we turn on a flashlight and shine its beam upward into a dark sky where does that light energy go? How is it reflected, refracted, or dispersed? When does it stop? What are the limits? While interesting questions, most of us get frustrated if we think too much about these possibilities. Remarkably, our thought energy is the same as this light energy. If we're bold, we can harness some of it for positive and purposeful results in our parenting role.

Our power of observation can be likened to being a flashlight with a strong beam that shines on each of our children. It enables us to see things more clearly, and when we see what's really happening and why, we're able to make wiser assessments and more realistic decisions about whether or not we should step into the situation or allow our children to work things out by themselves. Our goal is to help them grow and develop predictably and to increase the likelihood that they'll learn how to do more things for themselves from our modeling.

Clear Communication

Communication skills have never been in greater demand than in this modern age of high technology. There is more information available, and we know more of it than we could ever find with ease in books or by learning from communication with others. Yet, we still need to be able to convey what we think and feel in our relationships, or we'll find it increasingly difficult to socialize effectively and with satisfaction without hiding behind a computer, iPad or texting cellphone.

We send messages both verbally and nonverbally—verbally through either speech or the written word, and nonverbally through touch, eye contact, facial expressions, and what we call body language.

There is always a sender and a receiver in any form of communication. To send, we should say, write, or express through body language what we want or need with enough clarity to be understood. To receive, we'll need to actively listen to or read carefully enough to all verbal and nonverbal messages to suitably respond. Few of us would ignore or daydream while our boss is speaking to us. When we order a pizza, we make sure the clerk hears our topping requests accurately. At home, we need to use the same skills with our children and partner. What does our son's shrug or vacant stare mean? What does our daughter's pout or failure to meet our eyes when we're speaking to her mean? Why is our baby crying, when he's been fed and his diaper is dry? What instigates the continuous bickering between two of our three children? How do our children interpret our own body language or tone of voice? What is their response to our listening with only one ear and how does this affect our relationship?

To ensure our interchanges are correct for the situation and moment in time, we must confirm what was sent and received. There are few better examples of where precise communication is needed as much as with Air Traffic Control (ATC) and pilots of aircraft. Both parties are required to give a full identification of self and the other before communicating with each other. This is primarily because they're not making eye contact. When ATC personnel give a directive, they want a "read back" of the information they gave. Pilots can't just nod or shrug or say, "Roger," "Got it," "Uh-huh," or "Okay." They must develop the skill to implement proper verbiage. This takes active listening and clear speaking.

We can develop the same ATC skills when communicating with our children and ensure they develop them, too. This has never been more important than today, when our children rarely see us without a cellphone or iPad in our hands and receive only a modicum of our attention when they're speaking to us. They have quickly learned to emulate our behavior with their own cellphones and MP3 players or iPods and the plethora of other technical gadgets we've provided before they've even reached their early teens. According to a new study from Nielsen that analyzed the mobile data habits of more than 60,000 mobile subscribers and surveyed more than 3,000 teens during three months in 2010, our society has buried its collective head in various devises. The most disturbing data shows that the number of texts being sent is on the rise among teenagers age 13 to 17. According to Nielsen, the average teenager now sends 3,339 texts per month; that amounts to an amazing six per waking hour, day after day after day.

Although studies on the long-term affect of too much texting on health effects are still in progress, Sherry Turkle, a psychologist who is director of the Initiative on Technology and Self at the Massachusetts Institute of Technology, has conducted her own study of teenagers in the Boston area for several years. She feels the practice might be causing a shift in the way adolescents develop. "Among the jobs of adolescence are to separate from your parents and to find the peace and quiet to become the person you decide you want to be," she said. "Texting hits directly at both those jobs." It's difficult for them to grow into autonomous adults if technology makes staying in touch so easy. "Now you have adolescents who are texting their mothers 15 times a day, asking things like, 'Should I get the red shoes or the blue shoes?'" As for peace and quiet, she said, "If something next to you is vibrating every couple of minutes, it makes it very difficult to be in that state of mind. If you're being deluged by constant communication, the pressure to answer immediately is quite high." [http://www.nytimes.com/2009/05/26/health/26teen.html?scp=1&sq=MAY%2026,%202009&st=cse New York Times, Health section]

A reporter for the Orange County Register in California wrote in his column that his 13-year-old daughter had racked up 14,528 texts in one month. She would keep the phone on after going to bed. Finally, when her grades fell precipitously, he and his wife confiscated the phone. But as soon as her grades improved, she was given her phone again with instructions to limit her text messages to 5,000 per month and none between 9 p.m. and 6 a.m. on weekdays.

The young teen found an element of hypocrisy in the situation. Her mother was also addicted to using her iPhone, which she carried on her at all times. Professor Turkle commented on this situation, which is repeated in thousands of homes across the country. "Teens feel they are being punished for behavior in which their parents indulge," she said. "Even though they text 3,500 messages a week, when they walk out of their ballet lesson, they're upset to see their dad in the car on his BlackBerry. The fantasy of every adolescent is that the parent is there, waiting, expectant, completely there for them."

This situation is directly related to our becoming power parents. Our children should have our undivided attention when we're with them and we should have theirs. There are things we can do to ensure better and more effective communication. We might ask our kids to repeat their requests or comments. "Excuse me, could you repeat that?" We could also rephrase what we thought we heard. "Hmm, let's see, did I get that right? You said you don't have any homework tonight. Does that mean you've already completed it, or that your teachers didn't assign any?" "Are you saying you've already practiced your piano lesson for an hour today? I'm so sorry. I was outdoors and missed hearing you. Could you play something for me now?" "So ... Danny's mom said it's all right for you to spend the night with him this Friday because she'll be home to supervise. Do you have his home phone number? I'd like to call Mrs. Smith to confirm."

Sometimes, after we rephrase what we think we heard, the speaker hears it differently than intended and revises the statement. If we're speaking to one of our kids, it also helps to make eye contact and use his or her name. "Look at me, Michael, so I know I have your attention. After you've finished your homework and fed Fido, it's okay to ride your bike for an hour before supper. But stay within calling distance. Do you have any questions?" If we have a child who habitually "forgets" what we say, we might add, "Tell me what I just said."

We only have one mouth with which to speak, but two ears and two eyes. Some have said that means we should listen and watch twice as much as we speak. This seems to be true when we're attempting to communicate with our spouse or partner, and perhaps even more true with our children, who seem to be deaf to our voice on too many occasions. If we're busy doing all the talking when we're with them, we're not listening or learning. We can discover a great deal about ourselves and them from what we say and how we respond to each other. The volume and tone of our voices often say as much as the words we use and our children read a great deal into it. If we encourage honest and open expression of thoughts, we'll know how they feel about our parenting methods. They'll feel it's safe to inform us!

Our children also learn a great deal from what we *do* as parents. The old excuse, "Do as I say, not what I do," is no longer accepted. They learn to trust by watching us. They listen to what we say, but they're really studying our actions to see if we do what we say is important. Trust is behavioral.

Effective communication involves listening, speaking, clarifying, acknowledging, and then behaving consistently with the exchange. Experience seems to be our best teacher. We should never give up or become lackadaisical about learning to communicate clearly, both verbally and nonverbally.

Enthusiastic Experimentation

Experimentation involves the purposeful investigating of something new to us, with the intent of discovering or experiencing the results. This process requires exposure of sorts and is our natural way to learn. As adults, we do this all the time and have become more proficient over the years in designing and conducting our experiments.

We've all heard the saying, "The definition of stupidity is when we keep doing things the same way but expect different results." We may not be stupid, but we will certainly become increasingly frustrated if we keep parenting in the same way and fail to receive the results we want. We're not unlike a one-year-old child trying to place a square block into a round hole. When we combine strong will and stubbornness with repetition and rigidity, we've created that experience. The frustration occurs because we have the repetitive experience of failure. When our frustration finally motivates our trying something new (experimenting), we'll learn the value of flexibility as a parenting trait, because it can lead to more successful outcomes.

When that year-old child pushes the square block through the square hole and is successful, her natural tendency is to test it over and over again until it becomes a learned habit. Through repetition, she learns how to become adaptive and acquire the ability to change or modify her behavior to suit a new or different purpose. It's a natural inclination for her to learn anything and everything. We're never too old to use this system. Trying some other parenting method, and then repeating the best one until we get it right or are satisfied with the results of our efforts, is a good thing.

As we age, the demand for more complex experimentation increases in all phases of our life. If we haven't been trained well as a personal scientist during our early and ensuing childhood, we may become quite sloppy in our work and continuously experience overwhelming frustration. Our strong emotions, exhibited through anger, temper tantrums, crying jags, or throwing of objects, when combined with an increasing degree of difficulty and maladaptive personality traits, can produce ineffective experimenting most of the time. This tendency begins in early childhood. We bring some of our acquired frustration with trying new things into our adulthood and find ourselves confused and irritated by the retesting of our assumptions when they, ultimately, produce the same results. If such frustration arises over our current parenting methods, it can be devastating for our children and for us, but it's never a good idea to throw up our hands and give up. Parenting power comes to those who *don't* give up! If we patiently invest in becoming more effective personal scientists, even if we have a late start, we'll be able to help our children do the same.

We should encourage our children to experiment, too. Their family experiences are their first safe laboratory for developing effective work and coping skills that will get them through their school years and into a successful vocation. We must be their mentor or their shepherd. When they learn to trust themselves and us as their guide, they'll enjoy designing and implementing their own experiments. We can help them as they gain knowledge of the rules and how to control variables, so that when they get to the outcomes they'll have confidence in them. They'll have learned about valid and reliable results.

Persistent Plan Preparation

In the late 1950s and early 1960s, there was a popular TV sitcom named *The Dobie Gillis Show* or *The Many Loves of Dobie Gillis*. Dobie was a very polished lady's man, and his sidekick was this beatnik character named Maynard G. Krebs (Bob Denver, who was also Gilligan in *Gilligan's Island*). Whenever the word "work" was mentioned in any context, he would shriek, "Work?!" As a "hip dude," he had no use for this word or its behavioral equivalent.

This reminds me of my son when he was young. Anytime he heard the word "plan," he would cringe and say, "Plan?!" His aversion to this concept and its requirements were palpable. He was a laidback kid ... spontaneous. A kid whose motto was, "I just like to take it as it comes." It seemed to me he was operating on the principle that "hard work pays off in the future; avoidance of it pays off now." Many of us learn to avoid planning and, instead, practice avoidance until it becomes a habit or lifestyle that fails to serve us well over the long term.

I didn't learn to fly an airplane until I was in my forties. I thought I was already a fairly accomplished guy. Early after my first solo flight, I was practicing in the local area around San Antonio. Any new pilot can get lost fairly quickly when flying at 3,500 feet above the ground, especially when not paying careful attention to landmarks, headings and other references. Ultimately, if the pilot has a sectional map (I did), it doesn't take too much effort to find the location before having to radio that you're lost. Most guys—especially stubborn guys—never want to admit they're lost. I'm one of those guys. But, this time, the facts were overwhelmingly weighted in that direction. I was lost! During those lingering ten minutes, I had a very memorable set of emotions and thoughts that helped me reconsider the word "planning."

Having a plan is invaluable, regardless of the task. We may alter it, and usually do, but a good plan is comprised of logical thinking related to a set of circumstances. We get to choose a course that appears to be our best approach based upon the evidence. As a rule, we get to engage in this exercise when we're calm and can do a pretty good job of considering alternatives.

We're required to develop a business plan before starting a company and asking the bank for financial backing. This system works the same for us as parents. Having a plan for how we will parent and co-parent is worth the effort. We should first perform our due diligence and research and then define our roles as partners. Our definitions will likely be related to our strengths and weaknesses, but there are times when we'll need to be flexible and adaptive and take on our partner's role when the need arises.

In a discussion of how we want to parent our children, we should include what type of leadership or parenting style we'll use. Although there are many variations of styles, most professionals studying and writing about the subject return to three: authoritarian, permissive or assertive/democratic. Many times, we'll decide to parent just as our parents did, without giving it much thought, but the world has changed considerably in recent years, especially with cyber technology capable of taking over a few of our former responsibilities or becoming an increasingly easy "baby sitter." More than ever, making an informed and intentional decision about our family goals and values and how we can best go about instilling them is vital for the sake of our children and their futures.

First, we need to fully understand the characteristics of each parenting style, to determine which method we're currently using, the potential consequences, and whether we want to continue like we are.

<u>Authoritarian Parenting</u>: Authoritarian parents set strict and somewhat arbitrary rules in their attempt to keep order. They tend toward not expressing much warmth or positive emotion and are mostly concerned with being in command of every situation. In my practice, I've found that children of these parents usually describe them as controlling, critical, and insensitive. Most of their attention is placed on the "bad behavior" rather than the "positive behavior," so there's more punishment meted out than the rewarding of good choices.

In fact, children from homes with authoritarian parents seem to grow up with less ability to think for themselves and to make adaptive choices for the very reason that they're seldom given choices. Since they aren't provided with options, they aren't encouraged to think for themselves, resulting in their having less self-confidence, high self-esteem, or the ability to love and feel the love of others. This absence of self-worth is likely to transfer to their success in school and other endeavors. Why try, if their efforts are never good enough? Research suggests such children tend to be both more submissive and shy, or overly compliant, or even rebellious, often through extreme conduct.

Repeatedly, authoritarian parents use the well-known mottos "Do as I say, not as I do," or "Spare the rod and spoil the child."

And if their children question their rules and ask, "Why?" they're apt to hear, "Because I'm the boss and I said so." Too often, children who emulate their authoritarian parents imitate others as well, including less desirable peers, because they haven't learned to question the actions, weigh the various consequences, or set their own limits and personal standards.

But, if you currently use authoritarian parenting, you will most likely maintain control of your children and most situations that arise, at least until your children reach their teen years.

<u>Permissive Parenting:</u> Permissive parents are less likely to emphasize rules, civil laws, structure, or any of the principles needed for healthy living in a crowded and social world. They relinquish control to their children and avoid setting limits or following through with consequences of unacceptable behavior. They seldom, if ever, acknowledge the natural laws that govern our environment, our lives, and our relationships. They aren't particularly engaged in the parent-child relationship and aren't interested in actively teaching their children how to problem solve and make good and adaptive choices. They prefer to avoid confrontations of any kind and to not make demands that may not be followed. They want to be their children's friend and be "liked," so setting rules or limitations on behavior is contrary to their belief that their children will learn from the consequences of their own mistakes.

Research suggests that when permissive parents don't intervene, their children quickly learn that aggressiveness or being the "bully" is better than being passive. They act out in socially unacceptable ways and, later in life, find it more difficult to be a team player in the workforce, often because they haven't learned to set personal limits or to make wise choices.

If your parenting style is permissive, because you value nonconformity, your children may be creative free spirits who constantly surprise and challenge you. But, you will need to find a way to live in the midst of chronic chaos and to deal with the potential censure of others and the plethora of problems that may arise during every age of your maturing children.

<u>Democratic Parenting:</u> Democratic parents are interested in teaching their children how to "do it for themselves." They teach them how to be personally responsible and to consider the consequences of their choices. They have a warm, loving, and nurturing style of parenting. They set clear and reasonable expectations and give a realistic amount of time to complete tasks. Because they take the time to adequately explain themselves and give understandable reasons for their requests, they tend to be good teachers. They monitor their children to ensure they take responsibility for their actions, but they also look for opportunities to reward good and adaptive choices.

Providing our children with a few acceptable choices that are developmentally appropriate tends to promote autonomy and successful outcomes. Everyone wins. Research shows that the majority of children with democratic parents tend to be well developed, self-regulated, self-reliant, and have very positive outcomes.

We mustn't be discouraged if we find our parenting style isn't effective. When we find ourselves just trying to keep our heads above the waterline, we can stop and get out of the water for a while. Taking even an hour to think about and discuss what works and what doesn't work about our methods and then making a plan for improvement is a good beginning step. Choose the style and the approach that will produce the outcome you want.

Diligent Implementation

We shouldn't implement any new parenting plan until we've done our due diligence, that is, when we've developed a plan that reflects the values and principles we're committed to endorsing and enforcing. It'll be a plan that's the best one for us and for our family.

The plan will require our responsibility first, then the responsibility of our partner and our children. Accountability is the key. We must hold our self accountable, before we hold our partner and children accountable. And we must be conscientious about doing what we say we'll do and encourage the rest of our family to do the same. As we model our own responsibility and responsiveness, we'll be teaching them to trust us and showing them how to do the same.

Implementing a plan takes leadership and daily consideration. We must wake up each morning with determination to fulfill our plan and encourage every member of the family to do the same. We do this with a smile on our face and an expectation that it will bring success. This positive effort and style of implementing soon becomes infectious and habitual. It will come naturally and automatically, and it will take very little of our energy. Above all, we won't be like the individual who lived by the idiom, "If at first you don't succeed, destroy all evidence that you tried."

Larry Hays, a well-known Texas Tech University baseball coach, placed the following math statement on posters in the locker room and on the players' practice shirts: Attitude + Effort + Everyday = Success. Profound, isn't it? We are personally responsible for each element. Success is our choice and no one else's. When we have a good and sound parental game plan, and we add these other elements, we achieve SUCCESS.

Resolute Re-evaluation

A necessary skill for effective problem solving is re-evaluation. Certain aspects of a good plan remain constant, including basic principles, laws, values, and other constructs. For example, the natural laws of physics (gravity and aerodynamics) remain the same, but the elements of weather, the status of the aircraft, and the situational awareness of the pilot(s) are fluid variables. Once we've created our parenting plan, we must re-evaluate it within the context of changing dynamics.

Certain ideas we have about the way things work tend to stay fixed. But, what if our assumptions are erroneous? For example, what do we do when our three-year old son continues to dash into the street after we've told him time and again not to do this, because streets are for cars and speeding cars are dangerous? Each time our son repeats the forbidden excursion, we follow up with a stern talk and a "spanking" as well. We're confused as to why our son doesn't mind us and stop this perilous behavior. After all, we've accompanied the rescue with a punishment or *behavior extinguisher* that should prevent a repeat of the action. What child wants to be spanked? And why does our son seem to delight in scaring us?

The definition of a punishment is that it decreases the likelihood of a particular behavior from recurring. In fact, what we notice is that the spanking stops the behavior of dashing into the street for that moment in time, but it doesn't seem to discourage future happenings. It's almost as if our son is daring us to keep up our punishment plan. Or maybe he's thinking about the big hug that usually follows the spanking, as we assure him we don't want anything to happen to him because we love him.

As we resolutely re-evaluate our method, we decide that since the unwanted behavior (dashing into the street) remains the same or increases in frequency, the spanking is not an effective punishment or behavior extinguisher at all. Instead, it matches the definition of a *reinforcer*. That may not seem right, but it's true. We would not come to this realization unless we were observing, thinking rationally, and re-evaluating.

When our children are young, they lack the equipment necessary for resisting a high stimulus. They are impulsive. They tend to react without any "brakes." As the brain develops, in particular the frontal cortex, the braking function emerges. If our children are like little race cars, it's important for them to have brakes. This development unfolds in two parts. One is related to the brain developing and maturing, and the other part is a function of learning. Resolute re-evaluation, using this new information, can provide us with a more effective parenting method. We become our children's brakes. That means that we have to be vigilant every time we are near a street with our children. We teach them that streets are off limits, unless they are holding Mommy's or Daddy's hand. After stating the rule and then following up with the behavior over and over with frequent reinforcers, our children will eventually internalize this safety rule so that it comes under their own control.

There is a difference between using methods that are unsuccessful and inconsistent versus those that come about after using sound logic and re-evaluation and then changing our parenting course accordingly. In the latter, we make an informed choice that provides the desired correction and success. The former too often results in frustration, hostility, and failure ... over and over again.

Agreeable Adaptation

Developing an ability to adapt to change is another important skill we parents need. It's a personality characteristic found in most successful and well-adjusted individuals. It requires an informed flexibility in the way we go about "making things work." It's quite functional and practical. Rather than looking for the one sure-fire way to do something or using the method so-called experts say is the "correct" way, we look for what works in our family and complies with our values.

The more adaptive we become, the more resilient we are to little blips that are bound to occur.

Let's say, for the sake of argument, that our personality is the psychological equivalent of our biological immune system. It makes sense, then, that the more adaptive, flexible, resilient, and fortified our personality is, the healthier we'll be psychologically. We can fight off all kinds of unwanted effects on our mental and emotional health by developing a well-integrated and adaptive personality. Since our kids have a tendency to place great demands on us, we really need this skill! We typically suffer from this malady several times a week. It's known as *stress!* The more adaptive we become, the less we'll suffer from the effects of stress. The ability to adapt to all sorts of situations pays huge dividends.

Let's say we've made the decision that each of our kids needs to be involved in some sort of music activity in school ... the string orchestra, school band or choir. Maybe we played the tuba or violin when we were in school and know that our involvement had a positive impact on other areas our life. We benefited from becoming more disciplined and having a sense of accomplishment, even while we had fun and made several lasting and maturing relationships Since then, we've read of studies that show how involvement improves a student's dexterity, coordination, self-esteem, thinking and listening skills, self-discipline, and personal expression. On the other hand, what if involvement means our kids don't get home until close to suppertime and have to stay up later than their usual bedtime to complete homework? Besides losing a couple hours of needed sleep, they wake up tired and cranky. What then?

Adaptability is being flexible enough to stop, think, and evaluate. We can discuss each child's individual interest in continuing with participation, and if the desire is there, we can talk about what adjustments to their current schedule or work habits could be made to maintain the privilege and choice and incorporate more sleeping time. Or, we can decide to discontinue with the participation, if it's in the child's best interest, in order to provide more productive homework time and a restful evening. Each of us participates in the re-evaluation, and each of us agrees on the plan and the method of execution.

Relaxation and Recreation
Talking about relaxation and recreation in the same breath as learning to mindfully observe our kids, assess their behaviors and make rational judgments may seem laughable or more like winning the lottery, but it's equally important. Although we tend to think they're unattainable luxuries, they're necessary for most parents.

When we fly on a commercial airline, either the flight attendant or a video provides specifically voiced instructions for what to do in an emergency, especially when the result includes the loss of cabin pressure. "Place the oxygen mask over your face and breathe normally *before* you place the mask over your child's face." At first, we think this sounds selfish. Given more thought, we agree it makes perfect sense. We can't help our children, if we're not first taking care of ourselves. We can't help them, if we're unconscious.

The same principle must be applied at home. Our best self requires that we learn how to relax our body, soul, and mind on a daily basis in our home environment. That means we must develop habits that recreate our best health. This isn't a luxury; rather, it's a necessity. We should do this regularly, until our ability to relax is an ingrained habit.

Doesn't it seem a little silly to harp on our children to eat right, get enough sleep, and go outside to play and exercise, if we aren't doing the same things? Isn't this another example of "Do what I say, not what I do"? Sometimes, it seems easier to simply take on more and live in a default mode where we "suck it up" and run ourselves into the ground. It's easy to rationalize with that kind of thinking, because it's true. Many times, we do have to sacrifice our personal desires or needs for the sake of our children's. Parenting, more than any other occupation, requires sacrifice.

Keeping that in mind, we should remind ourselves that we're all expendable. What happens when we're injured or sick, out of town on business, or worse? Someone else has to take over. We have to use our resources and become adaptive. We have to streamline and cut down on activities. We have to ensure our family plan will work, despite setbacks or our active participation. We can implement an informed plan that promotes success even during a crisis. And sometimes we can avoid a crisis, if we learn to utilize relaxation and recreation.

While we're having our family-plan discussion with our partner and other support people, we can brainstorm about specific ways we can each be proactive in our effort to be our best for our family. The dialogue will most certainly include the skill of relaxation and recreation. When is the best time for Dad to enjoy his favorite pastime of tennis or golf? When is the best time for Mom to do the same, or to indulge in her personal passion of training for and running in marathons? When can we have "alone" time as adults, without our kids, to attend a play or concert or have dinner with friends?

We will live a life of enhanced personal quality, while teaching our children to do the same, if we incorporate personal relaxation and recreation into our family values plan. Nowadays, there are numerous activities available for harried parents who need time to relax and recuperate for the upcoming week. Here are just a few:

- Meditation, yoga, centered prayer
- Relaxation techniques, including deep breathing, imagery, muscle relaxation
- Reading for fun
- Massage, aroma therapy, sauna or steam room sessions

- Taking time for intimacy, romance and lovemaking
- Low impact exercise, like walking or swimming
- Hobbies and sports activities (painting, drawing, golf, tennis, horseback riding, biking)
- Good sleep hygiene 6-8 hours) regularly
- Your own quiet time-daily

Living in a Two-Story Universe

Early in my career, I had a wonderful mentor whose advice I valued. Dr. Hill, who is now deceased, described the way he viewed and thought about his world as living in a two-story universe. He went to the top floor every day to gain a proper and renewed perspective of it. The first floor was made up of everything he experienced through his five senses; everything was very concrete and linear, even the laws of nature. The second floor was made up of what he called the "Spiritual Realm" or what may also be called the "Quantum," a set of principles that attempted to describe what he couldn't see without helpful devices. This second floor, then, was related to everything that created the reality of his first floor.

I personally value this metaphor of a two-storied universe. There are so many dimensions to our lives. The higher we're able to climb to get perspective, the more we're able to understand who we are and what our individual responsibilities are. Climbing above the conflicts that invariably come with parenting allows us to see the big picture. We're able to catch a glimpse of the interrelatedness of everything we're trying to accomplish in our small part of the universe to the totality of it. It helps us appreciate experiences, such as shared joy; emotional attachment; sensing the pleasure or displeasure of a loved one; or even the power of prayer, good wishes, or a more positive philosophy and attitude. Parents need time alone to be self-indulgent and recoup for another day of parenting and shouldn't feel guilty while "relaxing" and participating in "recreation" without any kids in attendance.

An important component of our family plan should be how we can "tag-team" with our partner and kids, while each is getting some alone time. Sometimes, using other available resources, like grandparents, other family members, and friends (trade off) is part of the plan, in order to gain some of this "second-floor" perspective.

Even while we negotiate for alone time, we should never be forgetful of the difference between being personally accountable for our health and well-being and shirking our responsibility to our children and partner. We mustn't become known as someone who elevates our own needs above theirs as we develop our power parent skills.

Chapter 10
Principles of Development

FROM BIRTH TO death, we humans progress through developmental stages. All areas of our physical, mental, emotional and spiritual development are interrelated; they don't appear to occur in isolation. It's much like climbing a ladder. We advance at our own pace and may pause for a while, but we're always looking at that next rung on the ladder and are curious about what happens if we move on. We find that we want and/or need more than what we are experiencing. There are only statistical guidelines of ages when the accomplishment of these various milestones is achieved, but our development will advance due to an internal mechanism that is influenced by our environment.

Metamorphosis
As students in grade school, we learned that before a Monarch butterfly can emerge in all its colorful glory, it must advance through four stages: egg, caterpillar, chrysalis/cocoon, and finally the adult butterfly. All stages must be completed before the next one can take place. This is a natural cycle and the laws of nature regulate it. If we

observe the struggle of this creature during the end stage of metamorphosis and our emotions compel us to help it out, we would only be sealing its fate. The butterfly's struggle is necessary. Vital, life-giving secretions allow the caterpillar to become a fully developed adult Monarch. We can't tamper with this process. Someone once said, "You don't create a butterfly by pinning wings on a caterpillar."

The same is true for our children. Only when we nurture and guide them through each stage of struggle will they eventually emerge as fully developed adults. If we tamper with the natural process and remove barriers and responsibilities and do their work for them, we are surely sealing their fate. One of the toughest jobs of parenting is understanding the natural principles involved in order to help our children learn to do things on their own. Their struggles generate the metaphorical secretions of experience, knowledge, energy, motivation, and self-confidence, all which are necessary for creating a successful life cycle.

Listening And Letting Go
If our children could speak to us at the moment of their birth and tell us what they want and need the most from us, they might say something like this:

> "Form an emotional and physical bond to me so I can attach to you, love me, teach me to trust you, protect me and my rights, smile a lot with me, don't sweat the small stuff, safely expose me to all of the wonders of life, keep my laboratory safe ... but allow me to experiment and discover, and please help me and encourage me to always learn how to do it by myself."

Our relationships with them would likely change dramatically and in a more positive way. It's not too late. If we start today to become more observant, we'll see, hear, and feel that our children are still communicating their needs to us. They haven't stopped. We've just stopped paying close attention to them. They'll always want and need us in their life, but more at the front end and less as they develop their own skills. We sometimes excuse our decreasing involvement by saying, "I don't feel needed anymore." But, the problem may be that we're not fully involved in our own growth. If our children say, "Leave me alone! You're suffocating me!", then we're not fulfilling our proper role either. We're allowing ourselves to become dependent on our parenting role and not allowing our children to mature and do for themselves.

Let's be very clear, that's not healthy for us or them. Dependency violates the laws that govern nature. A dependency on our children will either reinforce their dependency on us, or it will reinforce their premature separation from us. Neither of the two are satisfactory outcomes. We must listen with both ears, act and react accordingly, and then let go as our children learn to do things for themselves

The Blastocyte

We are the biological product of our parents. We aren't clones, but we do share the same DNA. When the sperm and egg come together and unite, they form a Blastocyte, which is a single *un*differentiated embryonic cell. If it doesn't quickly and systematically start to differentiate, it will die. That one cell multiplies and becomes eye tissue, heart tissue, brain tissue, kidney tissue, and so on. There quickly develops an interdependency of these tissue cells that's necessary for complete health. While our biology and psychology are not equivalent, they are linked, and they do influence each other.

In a systems model, our family is like the body. To function in a healthy manner, every member must be differentiated, yet connected interdependently. There are similar rules of relationship that govern the balance and the dynamics of this connection. Flourishing families never occur randomly, just like biologically or psychologically healthy individuals don't occur randomly. They follow natural laws. We just need to recognize and monitor them and refrain from thinking we know better than nature itself. The minute we try to override the natural laws, we're creating unnatural consequences that lead us down the slippery slope of pain, destruction, and other unintended consequences.

Text Book Alert!!!
There are many theories regarding how we psychologically develop. For the sake of our discussion, let's use one of a well-known twentieth century pioneer in the field who wrote about eight stages of psychosocial development of people, from birth to death. His view was that this process is determined by the influences and interaction of our biology, psychology, and culture. He made two assumptions based on his observations of this process across cultures.

Assumption one is that as we progress through these eight stages, our world becomes larger. Assumption two is that our failures seem to accumulate.

Through our own observational experiences, we can readily confirm the first assumption. As we grow in size and age and develop more skills and knowledge, we take in more of our world, and our experience with it becomes larger and more complex. Without too much difficulty, we can find evidence to confirm the second assumption. For example, if we didn't successfully learn how to resolve conflicts with our siblings or friends when we were a kid or develop the personality traits we needed to deal with them, we've had to work much harder to overcome similar conflicts in our adult life.

According to this theory using the concept of ego development (*ego* is Latin for *self*), we humans move through a sequence of phases, each with its own specific psychological and social crisis. How we meet these specific crises is determined, to a great extent, on the effectiveness of our parents in guiding us to successful solutions—especially in the earlier years. Each phase or stage builds on the successful resolution of the previous stage's crisis. Without successful resolution, we're likely to experience reappearing problems. Let's briefly go through the stages, remembering that chronological age is less important than resolution of the crisis. Keep in mind that while our children are trying to navigate these stages successfully, we are challenged with our own psychosocial crisis (moving through our own stage, hopefully with successful resolution).

Stages
Infancy: (0 to 18 months)
Psychosocial Crisis: Trust v. Mistrust
Personality Strength: Hope

As parents or caretakers, we must meet the basic needs of our children. They are completely dependent on us for food, sustenance, and comfort during this stage. We provide them with warmth, regularity and consistency in routines, and dependable affection. They learn to trust us. They are eager students, and we meet the challenge of being eager teachers. Without trust, we encourage its negative opposite—mistrust. In this case, our children are incapable of having hope as a basic "personality strength."

Midway to later in this stage, we become aware that our children could become overly dependent on us. This is when we begin to encourage them to do things on their own. If we always feed them and always carry them, our over protectiveness may delay their ability to use a spoon or Sippy cup to feed themselves, or to crawl, then stand and walk. However, we recognize that we shouldn't abandon them and require them to always do everything on their own. They still need help, guidance, encouragement and praise. There is a need for balance. This is the stage where we do our bonding and attaching.

Toddler: (18 months to 3 years)
Psychosocial Crisis: Autonomy v. Shame, Doubt
Personality Strength: Will

During this stage, our children develop the ability to walk and to gain some control over their elimination functions. They begin to explore their surroundings in earnest. Our patience and encouragement are needed in great supply. Behaviors that remind us of this stage have a theme of autonomy or self-will: "Me do it," "My toy," and the abundantly used "No!" Resolution of this crisis develops a sense of autonomy (doing by myself) versus a sense of shame and self-doubt. When we reinforce autonomy, our children will more eagerly attempt new challenges. With the negative opposite—dependence—our children either avoid or are more reluctant to attempt new challenges. Self-doubt takes root. Trustful and autonomous children are ready to take on their world as it seems to get bigger.

Preschool: (3 to 6 years)
Psychosocial Crisis: Initiative v. Guilt
Personality Strength: Purpose

When our children have developed a sense of autonomy, they start to take on challenges that require planning and goal-directed behavior. It's no accident that this new behavior occurs in concert with their developing the frontal cortex (front part of the brain), which allows them to plan, and then to initiate or execute that plan in a purposeful manner. They are active and on the move. These are natural and "hard wired" characteristics that allow them to begin the process of mastering their world and developing a sense of purpose and judgment—the personality strengths for choosing a meaningful life. It's in this stage that our children get to experience their peers and other adults within the context of trust, will, and purpose. Smothering them with too much attention and coddling isn't wise.

"Good job. You're growing a brain!" I used to say to my kids when they were this age and in the process of doing something purposeful, like starting to dress themselves, tie their shoes, pour their milk, spill their milk (and then clean it up), use their words to get what they needed, learn the alphabet and ask "Why?" incessantly.

This is a busy and exciting time for both our children and for us. Our primary challenge is to use patience, to offer encouragement, and to be involved as their teacher and guide. Yes, it takes enormous energy to keep up with a preschooler, but, we're amply rewarded for our efforts. Since these years are a time of important play for them, we should play with them.

School Age: (6 to 12 years)

Psychosocial Crisis: Industry v. Inferiority

Personality Strength: Competence

This is the stage that leads up to puberty. Our kids are branching out and experiencing a good part of the day with others. We share our influence on them with other adults, primarily their teachers, coaches, and mentors. What may be even scarier is that their peers are having increasing influence in their lives. That's why it's so important for them to develop a strong sense of industry versus feelings of inferiority during this time when they're comparing themselves to their peers and siblings.

Teachers bear a greater responsibility in helping to assure that our children are exposed to methods that reinforce industrious behavior within the classroom, but we share that responsibility. Let's be perfectly clear, though. Ultimately, it's our children's responsibility to develop this sense of diligence or hard work.

Self-esteem is directly related to the resolution of this psychosocial crisis, and it's not a function of us as parents or our kids' teachers to tell them how special they are. Interests and activities, especially within the social context, become very important ways for them to develop competence. This is especially true if our children are struggling with academic performance. If both they and we are stressed with this process, we may need to seek professional help. We can request educational therapy or tutoring, if it's needed. If emotional and behavioral factors have become prominent, we should seek psychotherapy from an appropriate mental health provider for children.

Adolescence: (12 to 20ish years)

Psychosocial Crisis: Identity v. Role Confusion (Identity Crisis)
Personality Strength: Devotion and Fidelity

Hopefully, our children will have developed a strong sense of trust, will, purpose, and competence by the time they reach puberty. They will certainly need these strengths to take on this next stage. Erikson viewed the first four as dependent upon what is done to or with the child.

Stage five, however, depends on what our adolescents *choose* to do for themselves. Their world is, indeed, getting larger and much more complex. Adding to this challenge is the reality that they're neither a child nor an adult. This "no-man's land" is a tricky place to be while trying to define their identity. This is where choice and self-directed motivation become prominent in their daily lives. If we're not careful, we'll turn this period into a war of "control."

Our children are pulling away from us. Their need to differentiate becomes very observable. They are experimenting in a laboratory where the stakes are higher; we parents have less control over it, because it has expanded beyond the walls of our home. Our tendency may be to over-control, because of our own fears and our fear for them. We can have power over much of the consequences, but not over their choices. For this reason, we must become even more astute with our observation skills.

Monitoring and consulting are useful tools. This is a natural time for our adolescents to independently struggle with new demands. They must determine who they are, relative to their peers, and separate from us. Without good social connections, we can see how this task becomes almost impossible for them to achieve.

Our own skill set development of patience, encouragement, rational thinking, and effective management will be tested daily during this phase, but when our children emerge with a clearer sense of identity, they'll have learned how to commit to self. A devotion to self and the personality strength of fidelity is the core of any successful relationship. During this phase, they learn to trust themselves and to be trusted.

We will undoubtedly see avoidance of the details of reality and a tendency for our teens to be attracted to the "ideal." Why not? The ideal is free from conflict. It's easier to substitute ideals for experience. It's natural for our teens to gravitate to peer groups and causes at this time. More experience with independent problem solving helps them to embrace the real and practical world with the needed competence.

Adolescence is not a disease that will run its course; it just feels like it is. It's a "metamorphosis" much like that of the butterfly, and we must nurture this development. As our teens finish high school and move on to either college or the work force, we shouldn't give up on them—even at age twenty—if they haven't successfully resolved this psychosocial crisis of role confusion (personal identity). Many experts in human development argue that adolescence may linger until around age twenty-four, because of the additional demands of education and the complexity of our Western societies. Our early diligent and persistent work with the bonding-attachment process will pay out in "huge" dividends during this stage of our children's development.

Young Adulthood: (20ish to 35 years)
Psychosocial Crisis: Intimacy v. Isolation
Personality Strength: Love

Starting adulthood has much to do with developing a sense of intimacy in relationships through deep friendships, marriage, or committed romantic relationship. The idea of starting a family also comes to mind. With success, our young adult children can experience a strong sense of intimacy, because failure brings on isolation. All of this occurs at the same time they're choosing their vocational careers.

This can be such a stressful time of life for them. We experience *déjà vu* as we observe them trying to develop their own family. This is the time to remember that our first commitment is to our own partner. We must nurture the intimacy in this relationship every day, even as we help our children. They learn about relationships by watching us relate to each other as we connect to them as well.

Middle Adulthood: (35 to 55ish years)
Psychosocial Crisis: Generativity v. Stagnation
Personality Strength: Productivity and Care

During this phase of our life, we're busy raising our children, producing a work life or career and meaning in our activities. If we don't, we fail at passing on the best part of us through our family, community, and culture. We become self-absorbed and stagnate. Some of our children begin to leave us, and sometimes our spouse leaves us through death or divorce. We may lose our job and have to change careers.

If we're not successful during this stage, we're open to the existential "middle-life crisis" that we hear so much about. Depression, excess anxiety and worries, and/or abuse of alcohol or other drugs may be part of our stagnation and loss crisis. To care for our self and others in a meaningful and productive manner helps us to be prepared for grandparenthood and our legacy.

Late Adulthood: (55ish to Death)

Psychosocial Crisis: Integrity v. Despair
Personality Strength: Wisdom

Again, we mustn't get hung up on the ages associated with these stages of life. We're living longer these days and the complexities of modern life can stretch out the years of each of the crises. Chronologically, however, it's around this time that we've lived most of our years. We start to review our lives and, thankfully, most of us find peace and contentment with our journey thus far. We've had countless experiences and now have time to integrate them into a meaningful narrative. We have, and still are, playing multiple roles.

If we've developed our self into a person of integrity, we've acquired the wisdom to know that the world is much larger than we ever imagined. The Internet is swarming with endless information about every subject imaginable. It has brought this 'world' into our homes and within reach of our curiosity. Although we've learned a great deal, it's a proverbial 'drop in the bucket' compared to all there is to still discover. Nevertheless, our wisdom allows us to accept reality, and we're able to view our impending death as a natural part of our lifetime, just as birth is. If we fail to resolve this crisis in our lives, we're more likely to experience great despair about our choices. We may have no clear sense of purpose and may, ultimately, fear not only our perceived failures, but our inevitable death as well.

As stated near the beginning of this chapter, the purpose of reviewing the concept of ego development through each phase of our lives is to become more informed of the natural laws that govern them. Much of it is intuitive, but the subject is also well studied and has its validity and reliability in documented literature that has been tested and retested for generations. I like this quotation: "Change is inevitable ... except from vending machines."

We can begin right now to learn where we are in our personal journey. We can resolve various crises and develop the strengths we need to become more adaptive and flexible. If we're struggling with how to do this, we can ask for help and learn how to do it for ourselves.

Most importantly, as power parents, we must understand where our children are on this trip. They depend on our help to learn to do it for themselves. Any time we spend in thoughtful understanding of the phases of personal ego development will pay generous dividends for each of them and to all of us as a family.

Chapter 11
The Family Umbrella

Precursor To Behavior Management

BEFORE WE DISCUSS effective ways of managing the behavior of our children, let's review. We've spent some time contemplating how to take care of our self and our spousal or partner relationship. We've thought about how we want to relate to and parent our children and the skill set we need to pull it off. We have a basic understanding of human development and of what we need to be successful in each phase. We have also reviewed seven basic principles that provide guidance as we work toward becoming a Power Parent.

The relationships we form with each of our children are ours. How we relate and are connected determines the outcome of any sound behavior management plan. The bonding and attachment we've achieved during the first couple years of their lives forms the main support for our success. We can use a pictorial depiction of an umbrella as a metaphor for this statement.

Umbrella illustration with labeled sections: Development and Individual Differences • Positive Regard • Belief-Trust • Behavior Management Skills • Choice • Acceptance • Emotional Safety. The shaft is labeled: Relationship, Attachment/Bonding.

The shaft of the umbrella supports all the other necessary parts. To be an effective umbrella, every part must work together as a whole. The interconnection between these parts is supported by the shaft. The various parts cannot work willy-nilly, going in opposite directions, not opening or closing. If one metal rib or stretcher is broken, the umbrella doesn't work well. The section it supports causes the cloth to sag or hang flaccid, limiting our protection from the rain.

The umbrella of our family requires that every member work well together and value the core worth of the family, just as we do a well-functioning umbrella when it's raining. This is unlikely to happen without behavior management, because our children have difficulties with effective self-management. They are all too willing to impart their self-will and break the unity we're trying to uphold. The shaft might be strong, but if one or more ribs or stretchers are broken, we've got trouble.

How will our kids learn to do manage their behavior effectively by themselves? Their external environment will be slowly internalized over time, and, fortunately, we get to structure their environment in the way we want them to internalize it. There is great power in this privilege, and it can be accomplished in a very respectful and honorable way that always extends and honors individual choice.

Fairness

Some factors that are involved in our environmental structure are depicted as parts of the umbrella. Developmental and individual differences must be considered. We all deserve equal opportunity to life, liberty, and the pursuit of happiness. Nonetheless, we are not all equal. One of the most unfair things in this world is that unequal people are treated equally. Every human has the same unalienable (inherent, essential) rights. No one human has more worth or inherent value than anyone else. Yet, we are still not equal. It's an unnatural mistake to try to make this so. We live in diverse families and communities. A healthy society, however, depends on our ability to differentiate and still function well as a whole. So it is within our family unit and with our children. They have equal rights, but they aren't entirely equal.

Intuitively, we know this to be true. Let's say we have two identical twin sons who are eight years old. They share a bedroom. We give them both instructions to clean their room in the next fifteen minutes or they won't have permission to go outside and play with their friends. We return to check on them fifteen minutes later.

One of the twins has just finished picking up on his side of the room, and the other twin is playing on the floor with a toy and has not begun the cleaning of his side. We say, "Boys, since you are identical twins and we want to treat you equally, both of you have lost the privilege to play outside with your friends." If we put ourselves in the shoes of the twin who complied, we can feel the anger behind his protest. "That's not fair!"

This example about twin boys reminds me of a story about identical twin brothers. A certain couple had five-year-old identical twin sons who were complete opposites in personality, which caused no end of problems. Just before their sixth birthday, the parents decided to take them to see a child psychologist. The psychologist said, "What seems to be the problem?"

The dad said, "Doc, our sons are complete opposites. Timmy is always happy and optimistic. Nothing ever brings him down. Jimmy, however, is forever pessimistic and looks for the worst in every situation. He usually finds it. Nothing we do ever will cheer him up. We treat them the same. When one gets a ball, the other one does, too. It's hard for the boys to play together without constant arguing. It's driving us crazy. Can you just balance them up a little?"

The psychologist talked with the boys and observed them as they played together. "I see your problem," he said, finally. "Here's what I want you to do. For their sixth birthday, I want you to buy Jimmy all the presents you think he'd like. Don't hold back. Then go get a big pile of horse manure for Timmy."

"Horse manure?" Dad repeated, frowning.

"Yes, horse manure. Then place the presents in a big pile with a sign that says JIMMY in big letters. Next to it, place the pile of manure with a sign that says TIMMY. Wake them up on the morning of their sixth birthday and lead them to the two respective piles. Then watch what happens."

The parents were puzzled at this strange method of therapy, but complied. On the morning of their sons' sixth birthday, they led them to the two piles and watched with growing curiosity. Jimmy walked slowly toward the presents and started to open them. He said, "My friend has one of these and I hate playing with it. Why did you get this? I already have one! I hope you didn't get me a robot! You know I don't like this color. Do I have to keep opening all of these presents? There's too many."

Timmy, on the other hand, ran across the room and dived into the pile of manure. "You can't fool me!" he said. "Where there's manure, there's a pony!"

The story's moral? Because they are identical twins doesn't mean the boys are the same psychologically or that they have the same interests or view of their world. There's only so much we can do to help our kids develop optimism! Ultimately, they learn this by having a fair and predictable environment that delivers natural and logical consequences. They must choose their consequences. If we make the task of choosing for our children the focus of *our* life, we'll likely be continually disappointed and unhappy.

What does this mean? It means we should endeavor to live a productive and contented life ourselves, modeling for our children the way to create their own happiness. In this way, we add to the knowledge of our children's developmental status and individual differences. Then, when we add the strength of our bonding and attachment (our child-parent relationship), and structure their environment to be a microcosm of the natural world, we can mix together these factors and the seven guiding principles with constructs like the ones on the umbrella and have the very best chance of helping our children make adaptive choices for themselves.

Self-regulation is strengthened over time by positive regard; belief and trust; emotional safety; choice; and acceptance. Each of these is actually a great reinforcer of self-regulation. And each of these factors is derived from our guiding principles.

Positive regard is an attitude and a set of behaviors towards our children that confirms our respect for them. Even if they're disobeying us and need help with compliance, we treat them with the same reverence we'd want to receive from those who are correcting us. Our purpose is not to belittle or demean. It's always to facilitate their learning how to self-regulate and be more compliant and cooperative.

Positive regard provides our children with a context for developing a sense of emotional safety. They can make mistakes and someone will be there to help us learn from them, not hit them on the head (emotionally speaking) with their mistakes. When we create an emotionally safe home environment, we're able to nurture a positive and hopeful sense of well-being. It makes for a great learning environment and a safe laboratory. Our children can be like Timmy or Jimmy, an optimist or a pessimist, and it doesn't matter.

Belief in our children is something we give them for free. This is what we call "grace." It's part of that bond-attachment we've been discussing. Nothing can shake it or break it. Trust, on the other hand, is something our children must earn. It's behavioral and they must teach us to trust them, just like we must teach them to trust us. If we treat all people like they're equals, with regard to trust, it will be terribly unfair for them and for us, and we'll likely be disappointed. It isn't our *right* to be trusted, but it *is* our right to have the opportunity to teach others that we're trustworthy. That's fair!

Choice And Acceptance

Choice is one of the most superordinate (at the top) principles in anyone's life. If we think hard about what it means, we'll come to the conclusion that our choices have made us who we are today. We choose to remain in a relationship or not. We choose to cooperate or to be oppositional. We choose to be a law-abiding citizen or not. We choose to let others take away our rights or not. And even though we are more than our thoughts, we choose to think about all our experiences in a way that creates our reality. We choose to honor the choice of others, including our children. We choose to treat others the way we want to be treated.

All of us need and want acceptance, but our children depend on our acceptance so they can learn to accept themselves. Acceptance is non-judgmental. We can accept ourselves and others and still make judgments about the behavior of both. Let's say we have an adolescent child who is challenging us with seemingly endless talk about his values, which differ considerably from ours. Our acceptance of him and his choice to experiment with these new ideas becomes the embodiment of what is central in our relationship: respect. When we don't withdraw our acceptance, emotional safety, belief in and (maybe) trust, positive regard, or the honoring of his choice, he'll see that we're determined to maintain this rib in our family umbrella, that we're listening with both ears and responding in such a way that we can both focus more on this magical connection, even in the midst of our individual differences.

It's not an effortless or unproblematic undertaking to extend positive regard and respect to our children, in order to nurture their emotional safety. They need it for independent growth, but they can challenge what we believe are our limits on a daily basis. Acceptance of our kids is easy when their choices agree with our beliefs. It can be downright scary when their choices come into conflict with them. We dread the sinking feeling associated with our fear of losing them.

Our Heart Skips A Beat

Consider the story of a father passing by his son's bedroom. He was astonished to see that his son's bed was nicely made and everything was picked up and orderly. Then he saw an envelope propped against the pillow. It was addressed to "Dad." He tore open the envelope with trembling fingers and read the enclosed letter written in the recognized scrawl of his son.

> Dear Dad:
>
> I'm really sorry that I have to tell you this in a letter, but I wanted to avoid a heavy scene with Mom and you. I'm eloping with my new girlfriend Stacy. She's really great. I knew you wouldn't approve of her because of all her piercings, tattoos, and black leather clothes and the fact that she's older ... a lot older than I am. But I really dig her. We share something special, you know? She's pregnant, Dad. Stacy said we'll be happy and I believe her. I'm always on Cloud 9 when I'm with her. She owns a trailer in the woods and has

a stack of firewood for the whole winter, so we'll be fine. She's got a neat job at a tanning salon. Plus, Stacy has opened my eyes to the fact that marijuana doesn't really hurt anyone. We're planning to grow it for ourselves and also trading with all the other guys that live nearby. Oh, and also for all the people that use it for medicinal purposes. You can make a lot of money that way. It's a thriving business in California. In the meantime, we'll pray that science will find a cure for AIDS so Stacy can get better. She deserves it. Don't worry, Dad. I'm 16 and I know how to take care of myself. I'll get in touch with you soon and we'll drop by to visit so you and Mom can get to know your grandkid.

Love, your son Adam

PS: Dad, none of the above is true. I'm over at Tommy's house. I just wanted to remind you that there are worse things in life than a C- on a report card. It's in my center drawer. Love you. Call me when it's safe to come home.

What A Guy!

It's obvious to me that Adam gets it. He understands how important his family connection is to *him*. It's also a big plus that he's so clever and creative in how he reminds his dad of the importance of keeping everything in perspective (I love this kid!).

When our self-interest guides and informs our choices (and it does very naturally), we're able to fully understand the importance of our child-parent relationships. We're more interested in cooperating, when we appreciate the clear and valuable benefits in remaining connected. For this reason, we shouldn't dismiss and demonize the "self-interest" that comes with making choices. It's a construct of our natural laws. We can embrace it and use this principle with the other natural principles to build an effective family "umbrella" system.

Rights And Privileges

Early on, our children need to learn about rights and privileges. It's their *right* to be loved and taken care of by us, especially in their early years of life. At some point, however, these rights become a *privilege*. Being a part of a family requires cooperation from every member. Let's use the analogy of a school's football team. No team member who chooses to be uncooperative by skipping practices or always showing up late can demand to benefit from the team's winning the district or state championship. It's not going to happen! The coach will remove that kid from the team long before the championship game takes place. Obedience, respect, and willingness to put forth continual effort are required for a team to win games and championships. Rules are to be followed. It is a privilege to be a member of a team. It isn't a right. The ultimate natural consequence of being dropped from the team by choosing not to cooperate by flaunting team rules is the same one in a family. The natural consequence of choosing not to cooperate in our family should be to live somewhere other than with our family.

In my practice, I've learned this is the most difficult concept for parents to fully comprehend. If we truly value choice and someone—anyone—in our family chooses not to cooperate and scoffs at the principles of our family, then we must honor their choice to live outside of the family. As much as we like to avoid this topic, there must be an upper limit for choices. We cannot go past that ceiling.

There is no behavior management system that can be effective if the recipient refuses to play by the rules. This isn't "tough love." It may be tough-to-love, under these circumstances, but this is an example of the reality of natural laws. An individual's liberty cannot usurp the liberty of others. If we attempt to rewrite the laws of nature and substitute our own ideas, we will be laying the foundation for family pain and childhood pathology. Specifically, every family member will be made to hurt and suffer, but the child who refuses to cooperate will also be hurt and will suffer. We cannot allow this distortion of natural laws and expect a positive outcome. The answer is always the same: know the rules and play by them! It is a privilege to exercise our natural rights.

The Target

Effective and portable models help in our understanding of just about anything and they enable us to pick them up and take them with us. A target, for instance, has a center that we refer to as the "bull's-eye." Any time we're able to hit the target, it's better than missing it altogether or hitting it on an outer rim. We're aiming for the center when we play darts or when we shoot an arrow. When we think about our family unit, we identify the center of the target as our relationships and the outlying boundaries as our traditions, culture, policies, and behavioral expectations. Our motto would be, "Always focus on the bull's-eye. Keep the center firm/fixed and the periphery flexible."

When we're in a crisis situation, we tend to reverse this "motto." We move the relationship to the periphery and place the policies or behaviors or something else in the center. When we feel out of control, we tend to become the "controller." That has never worked in any kind of relationship. This is true, whether it's within our family, churches, synagogues, mosques, governments, or at work.

When we're in crisis, someone must remain calm and focused on the mission. Our mission, as a power parent, is to remain connected to our children and to use the strength of our connection to problem solve and learn from our experiences.

BULLSEYE: Relationship, Connection, and their natural laws

OUTER RING(S): Traditions, Culture, and Behavioral Controls

It is possible for our children to refuse to cooperate, even when they risk the loss of family benefits. This is true even in the extreme form ... being placed outside of the home. However, this possibility becomes less of a probability if we've laid the foundation of a valuable connection. When our children know there's much to be gained by cooperating, they'll also know there's much to lose by refusing to cooperate.

The clarity of the value and worth in our child-parent relationships helps us all make the adaptive choices that maintain a healthy family. A family that guarantees and preserves its members' unalienable (not to be separated, taken or given away) rights is a natural system that promotes prosperity and happiness.

As we think about effective ways to help manage the behavior of our children, we need to remember that the strength of the system we build will only be as strong as the foundation we lay. It is essential to build a solid and stable foundation for our connections. To be solid and stable, it must be reinforced with respect and acceptance and a sense of fairness regarding freedom of choice. Frequently!

Chapter 12
The Positive Opposite

Behavior Management Plan—Phase I

A POSITIVE REINFORCER is anything we apply or add to a behavior that increases the likelihood that the behavior will reoccur. A punisher or extinguisher is anything we apply to a behavior that decreases the likelihood of that behavior reoccurring. With children, the most powerful behavior management tool for a power parent is to reinforce or reward the "positive opposite" of the unwanted or maladaptive behavior. Dr. Alan Kazdin, former director of the Yale Child Study Center, is known for using this method with conduct disordered children.

This behavioral method helps us become proficient in not only identifying the unwanted behavior, but also its positive opposite. For example, if our child Suzie falls on the floor in an all-out screaming tantrum while we're at the check-out counter of a grocery store, because she wants candy and we say no, we tend to panic and look around to see how others are reacting. Some of us will pick up Suzie and sternly deliver a warning to her. "Stop crying right now or you can't come with me to the store anymore! You're disturbing all these nice people!" Some of us will buy the candy bar to stop the crying and the embarrassment. Others of us will turn with a face of chagrin and apologize to everyone, move our basket to the side of the line and ignore Suzie until she finally sees her antics aren't going to change our mind and stops crying. When Suzie runs out of gas, so to speak, she stops the behavior. This is a form of extinction. If we don't reinforce this unwanted behavior, it will *usually stop or be extinguished.* This is likely to take some time, however, and may not be practical. We need a better way to manage such a situation.

We could practice how we'll reward the positive opposite and shape the desired store behavior while we're at home. We could say, "Suzie, let's play a game. Let's say we're at the grocery store, and we've finally finished our shopping and reached the check-out counter. You beg me to buy you a candy bar, even though we had already talked about this before we entered the store. When I say no, you get really mad at me. You fall on the floor and kick and cry and scream that you hate me."

Suzie finds this game fun. She acts out her part, pretending to scream and cry and beg and hurl insults while writhing on the floor. We turn away from her, tap our foot and peer up at the ceiling. Then we respond, "Wow, Suzie, that performance deserves a trophy! Now, let's try it a different way. This time I want you to stand next to me and ask for a candy bar. When I say no, tug on my arm and whisper to me that you're really mad, but you don't hate me. Let's see what happens." Suzie acts out her new script with equal ease. Now we say, "I'm so proud of you. You knew exactly how to manage your anger. I like the way you did that. Here are two tokens (or bonus bucks) to add to your jar. Should we practice this game some more?" When Suzie is rewarded for her willingness to practice this new behavior, it soon becomes natural to her. When we go shopping with her, we keep tokens in our pocket to reward her positive behavior.

Token Economy

We adults work for rewards every day. We either work to earn a salary from our company or we work to earn payment for our services, whether we're an attorney, doctor, nurse, teacher, business tycoon or small business owner. We work to earn the accolades of fellow members of committees and even for our works of charity. Sometimes we're rewarded with trophies, too, or dinners in our honor. It's only natural our kids should earn something of value for their "work," in addition to our praise. Tokens can be anything that represents something of value to them. For example, we could use poker chips, marbles, Popsicle sticks, or "play money." We can be creative on our own or have our children come up with both the token object and a special name for it. Then we put together a reasonable economy system whereby the tokens are given a value and develop a menu of high-interest activities or special purchases that have a cost of "X" amount of tokens. This is a good way to encourage our children to work for them.

Now that they know what they are working for, our children are more willing to practice doing the positive opposite, and then make this their behavioral choice the next time they have an opportunity.

Let's say that Suzie wants a new doll or the newest video game. We tell her she has the opportunity to earn it by making good choices and receiving tokens. At first, we may need to shape this new 'positive opposite' behavior. For example, if Suzie starts to throw a temper tantrum, but catches herself and shows some ability to calm down, we would reward this with a token. Shaping—also called, using the successive approximation of the end goal—is very effective. We break down the desired behavior into "baby steps" and reinforce each step until we achieve the goal. We don't have to wait for the baby steps on changing every undesired behavior; we can use practice sessions of role playing to get there faster.

Cost Response

Let's go back to the checkout line with Suzie. She falls to the floor and starts one of her histrionic tantrums. One sure way to stop this unwanted behavior is to add an *aversive* stimulus, like electric shock! I'm just kidding, of course, but it makes a point. Adding a punisher that brings pain, like a spanking, can stop the unwanted behavior immediately. The problem is that it rarely becomes an effective way to sustain any *positive* change in behavior.

Another way to extinguish Suzie's tendency toward having tantrums, when she doesn't get her way, is to finish paying the clerk for the items we're purchasing, pick her up and walk outside. Then we remind her that she not only failed to earn tokens by her poor choice in behavior, she now has lost a token. This is called a *cost response* system. Suzie may become angrier the first couple times this occurs, so we'll need to think about how we'll handle this when in public, but finding a way to successfully remove her from the public situation will provide the best way to manage any outburst.

Cueing And Modeling

Cueing and modeling principles are also effective ways to develop new and desired behaviors. We can use cueing when our children are at a cross-road and need to choose a response that will get them what they need. By our using an effective sign, code, word, or "special look," they know this is the time to use the practiced behavior.

A cross-road for our Suzie may occur as we approach the checkout line at the grocery store. Let's say that we've already established the silent code of holding up two fingers in the commonly used position of the peace sign. We cue her that now is the time to practice the response that will deliver her desired consequence ... a token. After we flash the sign with a smile on our face, she has a choice to make. If she has already learned that the tokens can provide her with some freedom and the opportunity to go shopping for a much-desired toy, the incentive will align with her self-interest and she's likely to make the choice that will deliver. This is the natural way for her to learn our values. We immediately hand over the token with a smile and a quick hug or a "high five."

Modeling is also powerful. Our children are watching us, but many other important people as well. Their models can be cartoon characters, actors, and even sports stars. We can discuss with them how such people and characters model adaptive behaviors and point out how their choices lead the way to their desired outcome (what *they* wanted).

Three Principles For Strengthening A Response

After our children have achieved some success in developing a new adaptive behavior, we'll want to strengthen the new behavior. There are three effective principles to help us accomplish this goal.

1. <u>Intermittent Reward System:</u> Intermittent means that we don't reinforce the activity with a reward every time. We apply the reinforcement in a variable fashion by randomly changing the schedule of the reward to the second or third time we see the behavior, then perhaps the fifth time, then the very next time and so on.

    This variable ratio schedule of rewarding activities is the most strengthening reinforcement schedule we have; therefore, it is the most difficult to extinguish. For example, when we threaten with consequences and only follow through with them on a variable and intermittent schedule, our children's behavior is only variably reinforced. What this means, on a practical level, is that their avoidance or "tuning us out" behaviors become entrenched habits.

Another way to look at this scenario is that our children have placed *us* on a variable ratio schedule of reinforcement! We threaten and yell and get visibly frustrated, and they ignore us until we finally start to lose control of our emotions. Then they give in and comply with our wishes. Their behavior is actually a positive reinforcer for our threats and emotional lack of control. They have conditioned us to jump up and down and lose control. That's the kind of power we don't want to give them. See how natural these principles are and how quickly our children learn them? They work! If we understand the rules or principles, we can become proficient in using them in productive ways.

A variant of this first strengthening principle of intermittent rewards is the Decreasing Reinforcement Principle. We can gradually require more correct responses or a longer time period before we reinforce the behavior. We can slowly remove the use of tangible rewards for expected behaviors when we see the behavior becoming predictable. At first, we need to use these reinforcers liberally. These are not bribes. A bribe is when we offer something to encourage criminal or unethical behavior. We are simply using natural principles to help our children develop successful and adaptive behaviors that will help them live successful lives.

2. <u>Substitution Principle</u>: Sometimes reinforcers seem to lose their effect. In that case, we want to use the substitution principle, which means we present the old reinforcer and the new one as close as possible in time. After a few trials, we can just use the more effective reinforcer and drop the old and ineffective one. If, after experimenting with different choices, we learn that this method doesn't work, we

should drop it and stick with the reward tokens and just change the choices of activities or purchases the tokens will buy to those that are even more desirable.

3. <u>The Premack Principle known as "grandma's rule."</u> This is an important natural law. If we pair an unlikely behavior with one that is very likely, we'll increase the chances that the unlikely behavior will occur. This is quite simple and we can use it liberally. "Eat all your spinach, Peter, and then you may have some chocolate chip ice cream."

If we've made sure that Peter loves chocolate chip ice cream and only gets it when he earns it, he has plenty of self-motivation to choose to eat his spinach. Who knows, he might even develop an acquired taste for spinach because it's frequently associated with that wonderful chocolate chip ice cream. We can also try to stack the deck in our favor, by having someone that Peter holds in high esteem model that behavior for him. Someone like Grandpa!

Relationship + Expert Manager = Success

The first phase of successful behavior management requires that our children have a strong and special relationship in their lives; preferably starting with us, the parent. This is the support rod to the rest of these important natural principles and developmental needs. Our efforts toward becoming an expert in the use of "positive opposite" reinforcement and using the other well-tested behavioral principles will formulate the rest of our overall behavior management plan. As we become proficient and competent, we'll also become more patient and emotionally self-controlled. Everyone in our social environment will benefit from this growth, including our children and us.

Chapter 13
The Texas Three-Step

Behavior Management Plan—Phase II

IN THE SECOND phase of our behavior management plan, we'll learn how to integrate the ideas we've been discussing. We know now that it's our responsibility to manage ourselves first and then the environment of our family. We also know that we can't control the choices of our children, but we definitely have influence in our relationship with them, and we have knowledge of the natural laws or principles on which to base our decisions. If we focus on these truths, we're less likely to become obsessed with controlling our children, because they are the 'positive opposite' of controlling.

Here's another truth. If we're determined to focus on controlling our kids while they live at home with us, they'll likely focus a great amount of their energy into resisting our efforts. This isn't an efficient or productive use of our time. It's also contrary to our goal ... to encourage *self*-control.

Remember, our kids want to learn how to do things by themselves as much as we want them to do so, and they tend to internalize the structure and the principles we've placed in their external world. If we regulate it consistently and effectively, they'll internalize that regulation. This is what we call self-control, and we prize this learned skill above all others.

Since our main goal is to help our kids develop self-management skills, we need to target "compliance"; compliance is measurable. In any healthy family, it's essential to have competent and fair leaders and then to have the members cooperate or comply. Do you remember the example of the body being a compilation of differentiated tissue and organs that need to work together or cooperate in order to thrive? So it is with our family. If we parents are reasonable, fair, and consistent, our kids will be compliant and cooperative. If there's a breakdown in this system, we'll have the opposite of health and well-being, and our family will not do well.

Preparing For The Plan
Before we describe the system, there are a few things we'll need to acquire and a few terms we should define and understand.

First, we'll need a simple kitchen timer to carry with us. Second, we'll need a carpet remnant for each of our children, ages two through twelve. This carpet square becomes the portable and structured place where they will sit while being encouraged to "stop and think" about their choices. We can have them give the carpet a special name, for instance, magic carpet, think pad, time-out pad, or something similar. Its use is not meant for us to be emotionally punitive, although it may serve the function of an effective punisher in the strict sense of the word; rather, it is to provide a convenient and clearly understood place where our kids can sit and think about their choices and the likely consequences of them. Older kids can be put in a place of our choice, preferably not one where they will be distracted by others, games or objects considered fun. This is a time for contemplation.

The behavioral system we're developing is centered on the principles of freedom of choice, fairness, respect, and personal responsibility. Our consistency of efforts in keeping these principles as the focus is vital, so our kids will learn how to use them effectively.

Next, we need to "sterilize" our kids' rooms. By sterilize, I don't mean to scrub it down with antibacterial cleansers (well, unless you think it needs it). I mean we need to ensure there are no distracters present, like a TV set, a computer, portable games, music devices, iPads, iPhones, etc. We should place these devices in a neutral room, if at all possible. The reason is because we are in charge of the external environment, not our kids' choices. In order to control the environment, we'll need to be able to monitor and regulate access to these devices.

Our children's bedrooms will be a place for them to sleep, read, rest, and think. In general, it will be a place for them to be when they are on "shut-down." If children must share a bedroom, the situation just adds to our management challenge.

1, 2, 3, E.B.T. (The Texas Three-Step)

Once we've made our simple preparations and "sterilized" our children's rooms, we're ready to put our behavior system into action. There are only three simple steps.

<u>Step One</u>: We make eye contact and state our request in a very pleasant voice. We're a team. We give a reasonable amount of time to complete this request (set the table for supper; put your bike in the garage; put the Wii game away until your homework is finished; hang up your jacket and put your snow boots in the back entryway; take out the garbage; take your snack dishes to the kitchen; get off the phone and practice your cello/piano lesson). Then we say, "Thank you for your cooperation." We walk away and set a timer with a

reasonable amount of time for compliance. At the end of the allotted time, we check to see if the task has been completed. If it has, we say, "Thanks for listening. I really appreciate your cooperation." We smile and give a hug or a pat on the back.

<u>Step Two</u>: If the child didn't comply, we calmly state, "I'm now moving to Step Two. Go get your think pad, please." We place the carpet where we want it, ensuring it is out of the way of traffic or TV or any other action in the house. "I want you to sit and think about the choice you'd like to make so you can remain in control and on 'go status.' I'm setting the timer for two minutes." At the end of the two minutes, we return and repeat our original request. This time, however, we give less time—yet still reasonable—to comply. We restart the timer. At the end of the allotted time, we return. If there is compliance, we say, "Thank you for your cooperation. It sure is great when we work together as a team." We smile and provide a warm and sincere hug or a pat on the back.

<u>Step Three</u>: If the child chose not to comply a second time, we say, "Unfortunately, we have just moved to Step Three. You have earned an Early Bed Time (E.B.T.) because of the choice you made."

Generally, an E.B.T. is 30 minutes for children up to six or seven, and then it increases to one hour earlier to bed for children who are eight and older. Some parents choose to set the E.B.T. at 30 minutes, regardless of the child's age. In order for our children to owe a debt of early to bed, they must have a pre-determined bedtime. We should already have established a bedtime based on what is reasonable for each child and our family activities. This bedtime is firm, unless there are uncontrollable circumstances.

Honor Choice

In order for this system to remain philosophically consistent with the natural principles we've discussed in earlier chapters, we must honor our child's choice. This one aspect is the most difficult for many parents to embrace. The rule is that we don't try to make our kids comply with the E.B.T. We simply tell them that until they comply with paying back their debt, they will remain on "shut-down" and will not have access to their privileges. Privileges are the benefits we're given as part of cooperating with the family or team. It's quite logical, therefore, that if we're not cooperating, privileges will not be granted. Privileges include playing with certain toys, watching television, using the iPhone or Wii or spending the night with a friend or driving the family car. They will be different for each family.

Before we initiate our behavior management plan system, we should have a family meeting to describe the system and provide examples, keeping it uncomplicated. We could even write the system on a kitchen blackboard for easy reference. Then we follow through with the rules and consequences, until our kids learn how the system works for them through their experiences on a day to day basis.

Most of us have tried several approaches to managing behaviors at home. This one isn't just another attempt to try the latest and greatest. It's all about the *principles*. They are effective and, therefore, essential. The system will evolve with our increased skill and comfort with it. And everyone benefits. Consistent and united use by all caretakers will result in a turning point in the way we get along as a family. As power parents, we should be united in our resolve to take control of our home environment, because it provides increased time, energy, and peace. This is crucial. If we can't unite in this effort, we must at least agree that the one most invested will take charge of the experiment and the others will "do no harm" and try to be supportive.

Oh, Danny Boy

Let's say our son Danny is a 10 year-old with a long history of "zoning out" and failure to follow through with instructions. He's not a mean-spirited or malicious kid, but nevertheless, his behaviors tend to cause all kinds of problems for not only us and his siblings, but his teachers, friends and for him. His tendency to avoid, procrastinate, and literally not pay attention has especially driven his mother "nuts!" Danny may have become proficient in his use of avoidance as a defense against anxiety, frustration, negative thoughts about himself and others, and feelings of inadequacy. He has become an expert at conditioning just about everyone in his environment.

While avoidance can bring initial relief from negative feelings, it also creates great distress in that we never develop the skill to resolve the negative feelings, thereby becoming dependent on avoidance as our only option. Avoidance is also a passive resistance that can condition a response in others. For example, when Danny avoids, we complain and escalate his frustration with threats; then our frustration increases, prompting feelings of guilt and hopelessness and we have a tendency to excuse and do the task ourselves that Danny has been avoiding. Then we feel really ripped off and angry. It's a vicious cycle of mutual conditioning that keeps us both "stuck." While we're all caught up in this cycle, Danny may just be operating on the principle that, "The sooner you fall behind, the more time you'll have to catch up."

Our goal is to shape a different response in Danny and help him develop the skill to master the challenge that causes the emotional and behavioral reaction in the first place. We may say, "But, Danny has ADHD!" All right, but that isn't an excuse, it's just an explanation. We still need to help him learn a different and more adaptive response than avoidance.

Let's say we need Danny to turn off the TV and complete his homework. We might approach this longstanding problem this way. "Danny (while making eye contact), I need you to have the TV turned off and for you to be sitting at this table with all your materials ready to begin your homework in 10 minutes." We set the timer. Not another word. When the timer bell rings, we return to the table to see if Danny is seated and has his homework materials.

If Danny has complied, we smile and say, "Thanks, big guy! Now, what can I do to help you get started?" If Danny has not complied, we then ask him to retrieve his carpet and place it in the hallway where he needs to sit for two minutes while he thinks through his choices. We set the timer for another two minutes and leave the area. When the timer bell rings, we return to the carpet and make eye contact with Danny. "I need you to be at the table ready to start your homework in two minutes." We reset the timer. When the bell rings, we return to the table to see if Danny has complied. If yes, we use the same statement. "Thanks, big guy (or whatever is an appropriate and endearing name). Now, what can I do to help you get started?"

If Danny does not comply with the think-time or the redirection, we simply say, "You have just decided to move to Step Three, which is an E.B.T. (shut-down). I need you to go to your room. You'll still need to do your homework, but, as you know, that's your choice. If you choose *not* to do it, you will have to discuss that with your teacher."

Danny is on "shut-down," which means he has "zero access" to his privileges. Danny's earliest opportunity to choose to pay off this debt and remove himself from shut-down is later that night. If Danny's school-day bedtime is 9:00 P.M., then he must accomplish all of his nightly routines (shower, teeth brushed, reading, prayer time, etc.) and be in bed with the lights off at 8:00 P.M. Short of a family catastrophe, there are no exceptions. This is the logical consequence of the choice Danny made. The consequence needs to be firm and consistent, just like the consequences of gravity or other natural laws are.

If Danny chooses to pay his debt that night and does so successfully, we simply cross out his name on the calendar the next morning and he has a new day on full privileges. If he chooses not to pay off his debt that night, we leave his name on the calendar and he remains on shut-down the rest of this second day. He has the opportunity each evening to pay off his E.B.T. and to take charge of his consequences. His choice is his unalienable right. We must honor it, but remain in control of his consequences by following the system. This is a fair system that helps our children learn the principles and become better self-managers.

It's our children's right to have "Life, Liberty, and the pursuit of Happiness," not to have privileges. They earn privileges by living consistently with the laws of nature and logic. The relationship we have with our children is the "bulls-eye" on the target, and we always nurture it to the best of our ability. However, a *relationship* is two-sided and requires two separate responsibilities. Each individual is responsible *for* his/her choices. Each individual has a responsibility *to* the other person in the relationship. When we honor our responsibility for ourselves and to the others in our family, we're not only at peace with ourselves, we're modeling a healthy way to live for our children.

At bedtime, we may have a routine of reading, talking about the day, and saying a prayer with our children. Maybe we even give a short backrub! Such a ritual is a wonderful opportunity to connect and build memories. We should continue to do this even if our child is on "shut-down." The E.B.T. is not intended to be punitive in spirit. We're not trying to emotionally blackmail him/her into doing what we want. We must remove this fear mongering and control-type thinking from our mind. It creates terrible problems and it is neither natural nor successful.

Let's get back to Danny and his homework struggle. We must stay focused on the behavioral principles we've discussed. We don't resort to doing his homework for him; rather, we help him learn how to do it by himself. This is a good time to remember "grandma's rule" and how powerful positive reinforcement is in conditioning the desired response.

Who's Conditioning Who?
A newspaper cartoon depicted an adult standing near a doorway while observing a child in the corner of the room seated at a school-style desk. The child was peering down at the desk and avoiding eye-contact with the adult. The adult asked, "Have you learned your lesson?"

No response.

The next frame had a similar depiction; the adult was back. "Have you learned your lesson?"

Still no response.

This went on for about five or six more frames. The last frame had the adult asking, "Have you learned your lesson?"

The child raised his head in a glaring stare and said, "What do you think?"

The adult immediately responded, "Close enough!"

One interesting thing about behavior principles and natural laws is that they work both ways in a relationship. Our children are using them intuitively to condition us and their environment. When they use them with us, we call it "manipulation." When we use them, we call it "good parenting." The truth is that we're all manipulating. The difference is that when we use these principles to get what we want and we're not doing it at the expense of our kids, we're "manipulating with integrity."

One of our rights is to get what we need. We don't get to do that by denying the rights of others. That's hypocrisy and it's unfair, thus unsustainable. It's a behavior that is far from balance and harmony. Healthy and successful relationships with our children are created and sustained by becoming proficient in playing together by the rules. We win, they win, and the relationship wins when the needs of all of us are met, and we accomplish this by honoring the rights of others.

Managing the behaviors that support healthy relationships depends on having purpose in connecting, nurturing, and strengthening the connection. We also need to put in place a clear system or structure that helps hold us accountable to our principles. When we follow them, we'll have positive outcomes, but when we violate the laws, we'll experience the natural "negative consequences."

As we discussed earlier in the book, gravity is a natural law of physics. We learn this law all by ourselves, without a formal lesson or lecture. The fact that it is consistent and predictable, and that it delivers a negative consequence every single time makes it a good teacher. No one person is exempt from this law. That makes it fair. The learning principles surrounding this natural phenomenon are the foundation of our behavioral management system, which we call The TexasThree-Step or 1, 2, 3, E.B.T. There's no magic in the system. It's designed to be one of the simplest ways to help us become power parents by remaining accountable to the natural laws we've been describing. The power or "magic" comes with applying them consistently, like a good scientist.

Three-Step Review

1. Make eye contact with your child, and in a pleasant voice make your request. Provide a reasonable amount of time to accomplish the task. Set the timer and walk away. No debating. Return to assess. If the child complied, say something nice and encouraging to reinforce the compliance and cooperation.

2. If the child did not comply, move on to Step Two. Retrieve the carpet pad and place it in a location with no distracters. Set the timer for two minutes and walk away. Return and ask your child to complete your original request in a reasonably less amount of time as the first request. Set the timer and walk away. Return to assess whether there was compliance. If the child complied, say something nice and encouraging to reinforce the cooperation.
3. If the child refused to comply even after the "think-time," go immediately to Step Three. Say you are honoring his/her choice to go to Step Three. The child has earned an E.B.T. and will go immediately to his/her room and remain on "shut-down" for the remainder of the day. The debt can be paid that evening. The child does so by successfully taking care of nightly routines, turning off the lights and climbing into bed an hour earlier than usual. The child's willing participation in the system earns the right to be back on "go-status" and receive full privileges the next day.

Some of our children need help to learn this system. Ask them first if they'd like your help so they won't perceive it as nagging or controlling. Sometimes just a simple reminder about when they need to start getting ready for bed is the only cue they need. This system incorporates each of the seven guiding principles, but the hub is autonomy within the context of a secure and strong attachment.

Q & A

The following are examples of questions and answers that have come from my practice.

Q: At what age can we start using this plan?

A: The youngest age child that I've experienced benefiting from The Texas Three-Step is three years old. In all cases, these three-year-olds had older siblings who modeled the plan and they wanted to use it, too. Try it with your two-year-old … you may be surprised.

Q: What if we have plans to go to a movie, a game, or a birthday party and one or more of my children are on shut-down?

A: You must be responsible for deciding what constitutes privileges for your children. I personally considered these privileges and would get a sitter to watch my children and ensure they remained on shut-down. Shut-down isn't a punishment; it's just the natural or logical consequence of their choices. They need to see that everyone who cooperates gets to enjoy the privileges. Don't let their behavior punish you! Go to the movies!

Q: Can't we end up overusing E.B.T.'s?

A: If used correctly and reasonably, the system should accomplish your goal of increasing compliance. When it stops accomplishing that goal, you've overused it. So, yes, you can overuse it and you can use it as "just another" means of controlling your children, which will be a catalyst for more anger and resistance from them. Please don't do that. It is inconsistent with all of our seven guiding principles.

Q: What if our children get five or six E.B.T.'s in one day?

A: That's possible, especially when initiating the new system of behavior management. There's a point of diminishing returns. Use your good judgment; however, after two or three E.B.T.s, it would be wise to stop until the debt is paid off.

Q: What if we can't make our children stay away from their privileges? What do we do if their behavior doesn't change using this system? What if they are constantly out of control?

A: Some children are out of control, but if your consistent use of 1, 2, 3, E.B.T. along with ample reinforcement for the positive opposite is not effective, then your children cannot be managed in the home. They need to be in treatment and will likely be considered a good candidate for an inpatient behavioral hospital program.

Q: Will I need to teach our babysitter, their other parent (we're divorced), and their grandparents this system so we're consistent?

A: Yes. That's exactly what needs to happen. When your children see that all the important people in their life are on board with this system, they'll know it's important.

Q: Can it ever be too late to use this plan?

A: Yes, but only if your children aren't willing to remain in your family. As long as they see the benefits of remaining in the family, it's not too late.

Chapter 14
The Hybrid

Behavior Management Plan—Phase III

THERE ARE TIMES when we'll need to issue an E.B.T. immediately. Anytime our children violate principles of safety, mutual respect and our family values, they can be reminded of the importance of their choices by receiving an E.B.T. without more ado. Behaviors such as malicious lying to get someone in trouble, stealing, being disrespectful to a teacher, hitting, calling a parent a "bad" name (cursing), or any matter that is a safety issue and/or rises to the level of serious are all in this category. These behaviors need immediate consequences to bring effective correction.

The consequence is the teacher. This is no time for a lecture. When the dust settles, we can find ways to process or talk about the importance of safety, respect, honesty, trust, and so on. We power parents are charged with the responsibility to teach our children to do whatever is needed by themselves. As good teachers, we've learned there is a balance to what we say, do, and allow to occur naturally. When we can't allow a natural consequence because of safety, we substitute with a logical consequence.

Let's say five year-old Brandon has a penchant for walking out into the street whenever he plays in the front yard. A natural consequence is to allow a car to hit him. That's obviously unacceptable! Instead, we tell Brandon we know he loves to play with the other children in the front yard and we'd sure like him to be able to do so; but, until he learns to stay out of the street, he'll have to play in the back yard. Period.

An E.B.T. doesn't have to be the only logical consequence we use when our rules are broken. It does, however, effectively strengthen compliance and reinforce the personal responsibility of choice, as long as we don't overuse it. There are several other ways we can use logical consequences that are practical and specifically connected to the situation. As power parents, we need to mix it up. It helps us stay within our goals and to play by the rules, thereby avoiding fear, anger, and control battles. We do, though, need to learn how to "pick our battles," so to speak.

Even though managing and controlling our family environment is a demanding job, it's within our reach. Controlling our children's choices is never within our reach, and it generates conflict and negative emotions that will drain our energy. For this reason, it's good to know there's something redeeming and energizing about living consistently within our principles. When we're "running out of gas," it's time to work supportively with our partner to share the responsibility. Then we can stay relatively fresh and more composed.

Privileges

What exactly are our children's privileges? They'll be different for each of our families. They can be defined and formulated in a short private conversation with our partner, minus the kids. For example, is playing on a Little League baseball team a privilege? How about being part of the children's choir at our church? Although some evidence points to this type of activity being a privilege; we must determine this within the context of our family values. Like most matters of human behavior, there is no "cookie cutter" approach. There is no "one size fits all." Systems are flexible and principles are firm. As power parents, we must keep our systems consistent with our principles. That's the best we can do.

Let's say our son Chris, aged twelve, is a terrific baseball player. He's truly a gifted athlete and his team is depending on him to be the starting pitcher in Game 1 of their League Championship Series, a best-of-three series. They also depend on his batting expertise. He's a great hitter. Chris knows he's good, and he knows how much we want him to do well in baseball. He likes having them at games and having his dad as the team's coach.

But … Chris has been pushing the limits lately. He hasn't finished his required book report, and he's been giving some serious attitude of late. Knowing he's somewhat stressed, we've cut him slack and made it clear we're available to talk and help as we can. We've also made it clear that the book report *must* be completed before he can play in the game at seven o'clock the next night. He's known for weeks what the rule is, and all our efforts to use logical consequences have failed to reinforce better choices. A quick reminder that he'll only have about an hour to complete the report before he can leave for the game brings only a "Quit nagging me! I'll do it if I want."

The day of the game arrives. When Chris arrives home after school, his father is already home from work. He meets him at the door, makes eye contact and says, "Chris, I need you to have that book report completed by five o'clock." He walks away and sets the timer, ignoring Chris's attitude and the rolling of his eyes. When five o'clock arrives, he returns to see if Chris has completed his work. He's listening to music on his Mp3 player and hasn't even started. Dad says, "We're now on Step Two. I need you to take two minutes on the carpet to carefully think about your choice. A lot is riding on it."

Chris says, "You can't be serious! This is the most important game of my life. Why can't you and Mom get off my case?" He gets his carpet and plunks down on it with a snarling, "Whatever!"

Dad doesn't respond and sets the timer for two minutes. He returns and gives Chris thirty minutes to complete his task. He sets the timer and walks away.

At about that time, Mom calls to speak with Chris. "A lot of people are depending on you, son. I encourage you to choose wisely. I love you. See you in a little while."

When the timer goes off this time, Mom has arrived home and she confers with Dad to check on Chris's progress. He's lying on his bed and hasn't even attempted to complete his book report.

Now what? Do we follow through with our system (our game plan), or do we throw it out the window and give in to Chris's challenge?

We are the top executives of our family enterprise; that's why we get paid the big bucks! Tough decisions require a clear and accurate way of thinking and effective systems for managing. This is an extremely important time for us to teach the principles of nature. We have a great system in place that follows these laws, and it will be the superb teacher Chris needs at this time in his life—his choices have consequences.

Or, do we violate these laws and allow Chris to learn, erroneously, that he is exempt from the principles? This choice is tempting for us. We enjoy the compliments the parents of other team members give us. We dread having to explain why Chris isn't playing and know we'll be judged unfairly by most. And, after all, it *is* a championship series.

That's when we remind ourselves that the reason so many athletes in our society are in the news more often for their "bad" behavior than for their athletic prowess is because they were allowed to have an "exempt status" throughout their early years. They were conditioned to believe they were so special they didn't have to play by the same rules as the rest of us.

We decide family rules are more important than granting unearned privileges. "Son, the team will miss you." Dad says. "Your mother and I will miss seeing you play tonight. You've chosen an E.B.T. and shut-down. Consequently, you'll be staying home on 'shut-down status' with a sitter. We'll be going to your game without you."

Mom had already called John, a 20 year-old college student, and had him on standby. John is well versed in the 1, 2, 3, E.B.T. system and arrives in fifteen minutes. If Chris finishes his report and is in bed by exactly nine o'clock that evening, he'll have a new chance to get back in the game the next day. The rule must be followed strictly.

There is nothing I know of in my professional practice that will rival the powerful learning associated with the behavior management of Chris's experience. When his coaches and teachers remain faithful to a good plan that's anchored in well-tested principles like ours, we'll have presented life in a clear, natural, and predictable manner so that Chris can be certain about his choices and their consequences. No need for lectures. Being available to talk when he's ready is central to our relationship and to his development.

Personality Traits

Let's take that same scenario with Chris and make a few changes. We know Chris is a good kid for the most part, however, we've seen some disturbing changes in his attitude and in the way in which he treats others. Some of these self-centered, mean-spirited, and disrespectful behaviors remind us of a close relative. We know that genetics influences some of these characteristics, and we're concerned that he'll grow up to be like him. This type of scenario may challenge us to try to do more than we're able to do. We worry and become more controlling in an attempt to make Chris's undesirable traits go away.

Our personality traits are part biology (inherited) and part learned (acquired). We can't re-engineer the genetics, so our role is not to become a genetic engineer or to worry about it. We can, however, do something about our environment and take on the role of a shepherd, instead of an engineer. As we manage our environment and allow our children to experiment, the natural laws will reinforce the acquisition of behavioral traits that will effectively modify the biological traits. We can also model the adaptive traits we'd like our children to acquire.

Firefighters and rescuers are an interesting group of people. Biologically, they're "stimulus seekers." Some call similar individuals "adrenaline junkies." As children, these same people may be the kids who are climbing trees, jumping out of trees, or taking other risks that scare us to death. Without acquired psychological traits to modify these biological characteristics, we could have a child who's in constant danger, like a race car without brakes or maybe an unguided missile.

Part of developing brakes and/or a guidance system depends on proper development of the brain, but a bunch of it depends on our kids' learning a few adaptive traits, like patience, good judgment, self-control, the value of training and practice, working with a team, the ability to observe outcomes, and so many more. If these lessons aren't learned and the traits aren't developed, the biological traits are predominant and will lead to injuries, poor relationships, substance abuse, trouble with the law, and so forth. When the adaptive traits are developed, our kids have the opportunity to become special and gifted people whose traits serve them well in vocations that are valuable in a civilized world.

How does this apply to Chris's situation? Chris is struggling with making his biological traits work for him. He needs his environment to be clear, consistent, and well-grounded in natural principles. His journey will likely be fraught with more frustration than most of his peers, because of this strong genetic predisposition. What we want him to know, as loving and patient power parents, is that he can acquire new behaviors and gain control of them. His learned self-control can lead to a predictable and well-regulated life that also fulfills his physiological need for high stimulus and measured risk-taking.

We have to start somewhere, so the scenario involving his championship series is a good place to begin. We may think it's too late and lament to our partner, "We should have started this long ago!" We're correct about the value of beginning Chris's behavioral changes earlier, but that doesn't help the problem now. It's best to let go of what we didn't do and grab on to what we *can* do. We can still work the system and "fly the airplane."

Let's say that the scenario remains the same, except that Chris is caught up on his homework and other assigned chores. For some reason, he lets his impulsivity and disrespectful attitude take over on the day of his game and cusses out his mom. "You b*#&h, you're always annoying the s*#t out of me!"

What now? Do we chalk it up to his being an adolescent male with a lot of testosterone and poor impulse control? Do we rationalize, "We can't take away his outlet of baseball? He'll just get angrier and it'll make everything worse." Or, do we follow our game plan, because we know that our role demands that we are consistent and that his only chance to overcome these destructive traits is to learn to control himself, so that he can have positive outcomes? This kind of caustic, disrespectful, and destructive language has clear and natural consequences; and none of them are—nor should they be—good for any kind of relationship. Power parents never excuse this kind of behavior ... for anyone, including ourselves.

In this instance, we must follow the rules and give Chris the opportunity to learn for himself that he is in charge of his outcomes. "You have just earned an E.B.T., Chris. You'll be on shut-down the rest of the day. I'm truly sorry you won't have the privilege of playing with your team this evening. Maybe tomorrow will bring a different outcome, because of your new choices."

When this immediate crisis is over, we'll need to talk with Chris about the damage to the relationship he caused when he chose to speak to his mother with such disdain. It's not easily repaired. It's his job to repair the damage from his future choices, based upon the requirements we give him for restoring the relationship. If there is a willingness to do so and he has clear remorse for his behavior, then Chris probably deserves the opportunity to repair the mess he's made. If he does what's required, then he has taught us to trust his intention to cooperate with us in the relationship. If he doesn't repair the damage and continues to show this type of disrespect, his only chance to learn the consequences of his behavior is to find another place for him to live.

In learning how to become a power parent, so that we can create a healthy and happy family, we're not delving into individual and family psychotherapy or other clinical treatments. While there may be diagnosable and treatable mental disorders that contribute to Chris's behavior, we're not making excuses, only explanations in this book. If any of our children are exhibiting consistent unacceptable behaviors, we must seek out appropriate professional help when needed. However, we must also realize that even if they are suffering from depression or other mental disorders, their external structure needs to be managed according to these natural principles. They have considerable internal disorder, so they need external order and predictability.

The End Game

A huge influence on our willingness to remain consistent with our game plan is the looming fear of the "end game." What do we do if we've remained consistent with all of these principles and the results are still discouraging? What if Chris "digs in" and remains oppositional? Essentially, he's telling us that he won't cooperate, regardless of the consequences. This is *his* choice. End of story.

What now? We're back to the two clear choices that have and always will be in front of us. One, give in and try to re-write the rules, and in so doing, reinforce the notion that Chris is special and exempt from these principles. Or two, remain consistent with our well-developed game plan. If our children refuse to cooperate and choose not to be part of our family, they will not be able to enjoy the benefits or privileges of the family. We must find a suitable place for them to live while they decide what is important to them.

Saying Goodbye Sooner Than Expected

As parents, we have expectations that our children will be in our home at least until they are eighteen years old or when they finish high school. Then their exit is usually associated with college, work, military service, or something socially acceptable. Sometimes we have to nudge them out of the nest. We've all heard other parents tell of their experience of having to literally "kick them out of the nest" and hope they would fly. That's why it's such a shock to our expectations when our children choose to leave early through stubborn noncompliance.

There are only a small percentage of kids who push a parent to this edge and we certainly don't want to be among the statistics. However, this upper limit must be clearly established, if our relationship is to be sustainable and able to thrive. We can't force our will on our children and think they'll just willingly accept it. They must choose to be part of our family and choose to remain connected to us. Our goal is to do what we can do to make that an appealing and profitable choice. Most children will choose to stay in the game and get back on board with their choice to cooperate. The benefits are worth the effort for them.

Of the small percentage of kids who do force an early exit, most will learn from their experiences and make adaptive adjustments. If we find ourselves in this situation, we mustn't rob them from this self-learned lesson. Our next step is to do our homework and find a suitable and affordable placement. We can go online and research some of these places, call them and ask questions. We can also call a local behavioral or psychiatric hospital and ask to speak with a social worker who has experiences with these placements, or ask a counselor, psychologist, or psychiatrist to refer one to us. It may be helpful to talk with other parents who have been down this road.

Generally, placements fit into only a few categories. Certain relatives may have unique qualifications to take on this task, but this is rare and has its unique problems. The child's other parent in a divorce situation may be an option, but only if he or she is equally prepared to stick with a good game plan. Group homes are a good option for many children. Residential treatment facilities can be appropriate, as well as residential therapeutic ranches, schools, and wilderness programs. All of these require money and a commitment to a planned lifestyle that is consistent with our values and principles. All should have effective and knowledgeable consultants who can walk us through the process, if needed.

Defining our upper limit of tolerance is not a way of threatening our children to behave. It is no more a threat than earning a zero is for not turning in homework or earning an E.B.T. for noncompliance. These are merely consistent, logical, and natural consequences. As power parents, one of our most important tasks is to work with our partner on the due diligence necessary to define an upper limit;

then we won't need to panic when we find our child is pushing us to this ledge.

Our children will all leave home, eventually, unless there's a very unusual circumstance. They may leave prematurely, because they attend a boarding school that affords wonderful opportunities. They may leave for college at sixteen, because they graduate from high school early. Or, they may leave because of noncompliance to our family values. During their years in our home, we can provide the finest we have in an effort to create good memories and a joyful and meaningful life. We do this willingly and tirelessly, because we know it's our job to provide the best possible place for our children to develop into self-controlled individuals.

1, 2, 3, A.C.T. (The Texas Three-Step ... With A Hitch)

Once we and our children become proficient with the 1, 2, 3, E.B.T. system, we may want to try a few slight variations. For example, there are times when our children (especially our older children) are impulsive, or they give into a "bad mood" and choose not to be compliant. There's an activity they've planned for some time and they truly are sorry for their behavior. They've learned to take responsibility for their choices and they would like to demonstrate their willingness to cooperate and become a team player again. All of this is usually after experiencing an E.B.T. several times and learning the connection between choices and consequences.

We can use the Alternative Chore Time (A.C.T.) as the debt consequence. An A.C.T. can be completion of a chore chosen from a posted list, all of which take about an hour of hard work (or 30 minutes or whatever is appropriate for age and ability) to complete. These chores are alternative to the child's regular chores, but when completed will help the family.

In advance of initiating this system of debt repayment, we create the list with the help of our children. The various chores are age and developmentally appropriate. The details of each chore are discussed and thoroughly understood. Everyone knows what is expected to complete each task. The child with a debt to repay chooses the chore from this pre-approved menu. We give a reasonable time for completion. A haphazard effort won't be acceptable. If the task is completed to our reasonable expectation, the child has paid his or her debt and is back on full privileges. This is our child's choice. We must never take it away through force or coercion.

Our good judgment will be required as we determine when to use the A.C.T. instead of the E.B.T. Neither measure is meant to be punitive, rather a consequence that helps our children learn for themselves. They need to experience the consequence of losing privileges. Liberty only has meaning in the context of no liberty or tyranny.

Making Salad

Finally, it's time to make our best salad. If we've put in all the right ingredients, used the right proportions and added our best dressing, we'll have a pretty awesome creation. Some of us may think it's more like making sausage, but sausage can be good, too. It all depends on our perspective and the more we experiment and practice, the better the outcome.

We have, by now, developed several skills, learned some important behavioral principles, and put a system in place that will be easy to stick with, because it's soundly grounded in the laws of nature. We have created a safe laboratory for ourselves and for our children in which to "experiment with" and enjoy the exciting process. Creating a healthy family is definitely an adventure!

Relationship is the foundation supporting all else. Reinforcing the positive opposite is a powerful way to encourage adaptive choices. Consistent use of a well-developed and philosophically sound system that requires very little administrative resources will be the best that we can do to provide "top notch" management for our family.

Chapter 15
One-Way Trip with Our Memories Meter Ticking

EVERY MEMBER OF our family is on a one-way trip into the future. While we don't get to, literally, return to where we departed, we do get to pull over and make sure we know where we're going. For this reason, we need to be clear about our destination and consider that when we arrive at our final destination, we will have created many memories.

That "memories meter" is always ticking and memories will be created, whether intentionally or unintentionally. When we power parents finally arrive at our destination, it's our great hope that we'll have helped create at least two positive memories for every negative one, and our children will view their history with us in affirmative terms. Two to one isn't all that bad. However, the more we can increase that ratio, the better.

Some time ago, I was enjoying a very nice meal with my wife at one of our favorite lunch spots. As is our tradition, we opened our fortune cookies. The one I remember to this day is hers. One of the reasons I remember hers and not mine is that it was so "her." The other reason is that it was one of the best fortunes from a fortune cookie I've ever read. It said, "Sweet memories are the paradise of the mind."

Not all of our experiences will seem sweet, but when a negative one occurs, it can bring about a positive outcome. Just as gravity has its negatives, it also has positives. Without gravity, we wouldn't have the resistance required to strengthen the muscles that allow us to walk or run. The monarch butterfly is able to secrete fluids that promote vigor and health only because it goes through adversity. The memories we create with our children, when we model a positive and "can do" attitude, will last forever with them. This attitude is contagious and there's strength and support in numbers. As our family pulls together under adversity, positive outcomes are bound to follow.

What constitutes good memories? If we do some inventive thinking, we'll be able to come up with a few ideas for the memories we'd like our kids to have of their childhood in our home. Vacations, birthdays, holidays, one-on-one times, special traditions, and night time routines can all become special experiences that generate these positive reminiscences. Repeating with our children some of our favorite family experiences when we were kids is a way to introduce lasting traditions. All three generations from both sides of the family can participate in conversation and laughter as each memory is recalled and revived. Our children get a kick out of learning about our mistakes and successes when we were their age and then imparting their personal stamp that results in improving the ongoing "story."

One of the many things I love about my wife is that she believes in this positive memory-making responsibility. She's good at it, too. When our children were just babies, she habitually stood in front of a mirror while holding and hugging them. She continued with this tradition until … well, now! To this day, she will hug our adult children in front of a mirror so they experience not only the tactile and emotional feel of the hug, but also get to see it. It creates a multi-sensory memory. Guess who gets the same treatment? That's right, our grandkids. And guess who continues the tradition for her children? Right again, our daughter.

We may not have the resources to travel to exotic places or to expose our children to all of the fine things in our world, but we all can create our own family traditions whose memories will last a lifetime. Our memories become the representation of our life together. We have the power to script the story of our family. What fills our memories is very powerful. "Our sweet memories are the paradise of our minds."

The impact of these memories is mutual, because of our connection. I remember back in those early years of our children—while in graduate school—walking downtown on the cobblestone streets on a cold day. We would walk to a small market that sold fresh produce from the local farmers. We pulled the kids in a red wagon. There was a man that had a bicycle with a knapsack attached with all of his belongings. We had seen him many times before. Our daughter was about five-and-a-half, so that would make our son about two-and-a-half. We saw her staring at the man and as we gently turned her head back to us, she said she was sad because the man didn't have a coat and it was very cold. She was worried that he would get sick and die!

The sadder she became, the sadder her brother became. Before long, they were both crying and we had to pull them over to the side and try to console them. Well, they were always taught to be kind and helpful to others—especially those who were in need, they seemed to be inconsolable. Now, we could have tried to explain that we didn't have much either, but you know how that would have gone over. Kids are too smart for some rationalizations. It was obvious to them that I had more than one coat, and the poor man didn't seem to have any coat. Yep, you know what happened next!

The only thing that would console them is for me to give the man my coat. That was a bit awkward. As I tried to come up with a way to offer my coat, my daughter said, "Daddy, why don't you leave your coat on his bicycle so he want be embarrassed?" What a memory; and what a lesson—for me! The lesson I learned from my children that day kept me warm on the walk back home. In fact, it warms me every time I remember it and it's a great example of how the mutuality principle works.

About a year later, our family was returning from a trip to San Antonio for a family visit. We were headed north on IH 35 and it was raining, "big time." Warm and toasty, in our 1979 VW Bus, we were driving very slowly and carefully as the wipers worked rapidly and rhythmically as the heater was blasting and we peered out the window to see the road. Up ahead, on the side of the highway, a young man was walking in the cold rain—*without a coat*. Sound familiar? Two little kid's faces were smashed into the side window staring at the young man.

Well, you can imagine the conversation. "Daddy, you have to stop and pick him up! He's going to get sick. He's cold. You have to do something!" Then … a flood of tears. I took the next exit and pulled over. Here we were, in the evening, with two small children and a long road ahead. What do we do, as there were legitimate safety concerns? We tried to talk about safety and all of that stuff, but got nowhere with that line of reasoning with our two kids. So, we turned around remaining on the access road until the next underpass.

Under-and-around we went until we were back on our northbound route. Sure enough, the young man was still walking slowly into the chilly north rain. We stopped and slid-open the side door and invited him into the warm dry bus. I'll never forget the look on the kid's and the young man's faces. All three had huge smiles. About ten miles up the road we turned off the highway and took this young man to his house.

He was about as grateful as you could ever expect someone to be. But, I think we were more grateful for that memory than he may have been for the ride on that cold rainy day. We successfully completed that long trip with two very happy children and we've replayed that day together many times over the past thirty years. Recalling great memories always generates a smile on our faces with meaningful conversations.

Children are intuitive and sensitive beings that have memories like elephants. We can learn a lot from them. We'll never regret the time, energy and money we choose to invest in happy and memorable times. In this day of digital cameras and iPads, we can easily and visually document literally hundreds of cherished moments for many generations to come.

Our legacy is to leave *our self* with our children and grandchildren. All of our values and principles, all of our tenderness and encouragement, all of our love and goodness will be passed on generation after generation through our children ... if we've purposefully made the decision to become a power parent, in order to create a healthy family. Generate, at the least, a two-to-one ratio of positive versus negative memories with your children. They will be "the paradise of your mind!"

Epilogue
Quick Reference and Review

THIS LAST CHAPTER is designed to provide you with a quick reference in a chapter outline format. Hopefully, you will return many times to review this information as you refine and strengthen your power-parent skills.

Part I: The Seven Principles

Chapter 1: Attachment Principle

- The parent-child attachment process is natural and follows certain rules. It begins from the moment our children are born into this world.
- We parents are in charge of bonding with our children, and we must choose to behave in an organized and predictable manner if our children are to learn how to develop a secure attachment. The process takes work and will require our availability and accessibility.
- We must balance our behaviors with developing a secure base and encouraging safe self-exploration. Recognizing

and developing sophistication with our own internal working model is an immense help in the attachment process, as our working model expresses our own pattern of attachment and this can predict that of our children.
- We are the primary teachers of our children. When they are securely attached to us, their learning becomes more expansive and efficient.
- All of our effective daily management of our family environment and family relationship is hinged to the attachment principle. Because we are securely connected, we have a great deal to loose. Hence, we have greater motivation to cooperate and remain connected as a healthy family.
- Attachment is the first principle of the Power Parent.

Chapter 2: Autonomy Principle

- Autonomy = Sovereignty = Supreme Power.
- Our supreme power is our freedom to choose.
- Since each of us has this unalienable right of choice, so do our children.
- We parents are responsible for helping our children make adaptive choices.
- Ultimately, we parents are like a lighthouse; we light the way for our children.
- We parents create a safe laboratory and help prepare good scientists.
- We must remain steadfast, strong and unwavering in the midst of chaos.

Chapter 3: Balance Principle

- Balance is the principle that helps create stability.
- Self-regulation and adaptation are included within the balance principle and help create the positive effects of this law.
- Denial/avoidance and the absence of adaptability are also included and create the negative effects of this law.
- Healthy balance requires holding on to valid outcomes and letting go of invalid outcomes.
- Flexibility is included within the balance principle.
- Principles are hierarchical (placed on a ladder) and are arranged as superordinate to subordinate (highest to lowest).

Chapter 4: Bipolarity Principle

- Most, if not all constructs are bipolar (two poles).
- Mutual exclusivity is included within the bipolarity principle (if one, then not the other).
- We can't be relaxed and tense at the same time.
- The brain operates on positive feedback only.
- Rewarding the positive opposite is a powerful behavior management tool.
- Our sovereign right to choose how to think allows us to develop characteristics of our personality over time, pervasively either positive or negative.

Chapter 5: Mutuality Principle

- Mutuality requires interdependency.

- Interdependency requires responsibility for self and responsibility to others.
- "I can do it for myself" evolves into "I can do for others."
- The essence of the mutuality principle is the Golden Rule.
- The Golden Rule is active; we must look for ways to treat others as we wish to be treated.
- Autonomy is necessary, but not sufficient. Mutuality is also required.
- The mutuality principle gives birth to the most powerful force known to humanity: Love.

Chapter 6: Reinforcement Principle

- Reinforcement is anything we add after a behavior occurs that increases the likelihood of the behavior reoccurring in the future.
- Negative reinforcement is anything we remove after a behavior occurs that increases the likelihood of that behavior reoccurring in the future.
- Punishment is any measure we take after a behavior occurs, which decreases the likelihood of that behavior reoccurring in the future.
- Negative punishment is any measure we take and remove after a behavior occurs that decreases the likelihood of that behavior reoccurring in the future.
- Valence is a psychological value placed on anything (pleasurable or aversive).
- Behaviors have three parts: (A, B, C) Antecedent, Behavior, and Consequence.

- A double barreled consequence is negative punishment and positive reinforcement.
- Self-reinforcement can be as powerful as external reinforcement.
- Grandma's Rule: Any high-frequency activities (eating ice cream) can be used to reinforce any low-frequency activities (eating spinach).
- Modify the antecedent and the consequence and the behavior will change.
- We parents must be responsible for the environment (the antecedent and the consequence) and our children must be responsible for the behavior.

Chapter 7: Parsimony Principle

- Keep It Simple Stupid (KISS).
- The simplest explanation is usually the best.
- Occam's razor: Shave away everything that is not needed.
- Simplicity allows us to work our plan with consistency.

Part II: Putting the Principles to Work

Chapter 8: The Starting Line

- Patience balances emotions.
- Our thoughts are the regulators of our emotions.
- We must shake it off and step up; attitude is everything.
- We are our own personal scientist and must be the best we can be.

- We must emotionally bond with our children so they can attach to us.
- We must fly the airplane when in a crisis and remain focused on our primary job.
- We must continuously practice and develop our parenting skills.
- Our children's safety and happiness depends our working well with our spouse/partner to teach our children to do it for themselves.

Chapter 9: Power-Parent Skills

- <u>Mindful Observation</u>: Be aware and pay attention to the things we value.
- <u>Accurate Assessment</u>: Assess frequently and make adjustments to get back on our course ASAP.
- <u>Rational Judgment and Perception</u>: Use the power of purposeful and rational thinking to help regulate our emotional experiences.
- <u>Clear Communication</u>: Effective communication involves listening, speaking, clarifying, acknowledging, and then behaving consistently with the exchange.
- <u>Enthusiastic Experimentation</u>: If we invest in becoming good and effective scientists, we'll be able to help our children do the same. We should encourage experimenting.
- <u>Persistent Plan Preparation</u>: Rather than repeating what our parents did without giving it much thought; we should develop our own plan and parenting style:

- <u>Authoritarian Style</u>: Concern is controlling; children tend to be either submissive or rebellious.
- <u>Permissive Style</u>: No emphasis on principles necessary for healthy living: children tend to be aggressive and act out.
- <u>Democratic</u>: Interested in teaching children to do for themselves; children tend to be well-developed, self-regulated and self-reliant.
- <u>Diligent Implementation</u>: Leadership and daily diligence are needed to implement a plan. Attitude + Effort + Everyday = Success.
- <u>Resolute Reevaluation</u>: Follow the natural laws and observe the outcome of what we add or take away related to our children's choices. Make sure the outcome is what we intended. If not, change the consequence to reinforce or punish (extinguish) the maladaptive choice of our child. Appropriate correction brings success.
- <u>Agreeable Adaptation</u>: Being flexible enough to find good outcomes that are naturally strengthened and become habitual. Adaptability strengthens resilience.
- <u>Relaxation and Recreation</u>: Our best self requires that we know how to relax our body, soul, and mind and develop habits that recreate our best health. We live in a "two-story" universe and can't avoid or deny either the first- or second-floor responsibilities. Our metaphysical/spiritual principles give meaning and purpose to the physical principles. We must find our way back up the stairs to the second floor and spend quality time developing these skills.

Chapter 10: Principles of Development

- "We don't create a butterfly by pinning wings on a caterpillar." Development is an internal mechanism influenced by the environment.
- Individuals must differentiate from their family of origin, just like the cells of the Blastocyte must differentiate in order to have a healthy body. Autonomy and mutuality require this development.

1. Infancy (0 to18 months): Psychosocial Crises: Trust v. Mistrust; Personality Strength: Hope
2. Toddler (18 months to 3 years): Psychosocial Crises: Autonomy v. Shame, Doubt; Personality Strength: Will
3. Preschool (3 to 6 years): Psychosocial Crises: Initiative v. Guilt; Personality Strength: Purpose
4. School Age (6 to 12 years): Psychosocial Crises: Industry v. Inferiority: Personality Strength: Competence
5. Adolescence (12 to 20ish years): Psychosocial Crises: Identity v. Role Confusion (Identity Crises); Personality Strength: Devotion and Fidelity
6. Young Adult (20ish to 35 years): Psychosocial Crises: Intimacy v. Isolation; Personality Strength: Love
7. Middle Adulthood (35 to 55ish): Psychosocial Crises: Generativity v. Stagnation; Personality Strength: Productivity and Care
8. Late Adulthood (55ish to Death): Psychosocial Crises: Integrity v. Despair; Personality Strength: Wisdom

Chapter 11: The Family Umbrella

- The power parent's behavior management is like a good working umbrella. It has many parts supported by the "shaft" (the relationship we have created with our children). Each part must be securely connected to the shaft with integrity, in order to be functional.
- It is unfair that unequal people are treated equally. Our rights are equal, our privileges are not; we earn those.
- Choice is inherent in our autonomy.
- Unalienable rights are extended to all; privileges are earned.
- Remember the target. Keep the bulls-eye (relationship) firm and the peripheral part of the target (traditions, cultural factors, arbitrary guidelines) flexible.

Chapter 12: The Positive Opposite

- Identify and reinforce the positive opposite.
- Model and practice the desired behavior/skill. Use cueing when a child is at a cross-road and needs to choose wisely. Cue up the modeled and practiced behavior.
- The variable ratio schedule of rewarding activities is the most strengthening reinforcement schedule we have. The "Decreasing Reinforcement Principle" is a variant of the variable ratio. Try gradually requiring more tokens or correct responses or a longer time period before you reward a behavior. This tact strengthens the desired behavior.
- The Substitution Principle is used when a child seems to lose interest in something that used to be rewarding. It allows us to pair the old reinforcer with a new reinforcer

and, in time, we can drop the old one for the new and more effective one. We can also attach a reward with higher value to earned tokens. Children will continue to work hard to earn tokens that will be redeemed for a highly rewarding privilege.
- Use Grandma's Rule: "Eat your spinach and then you get your ice cream."
- Relationship + Expert Manager = Success.

Chapter 13: The Texas Three-Step

- Encourage children to do it by themselves.
- Use a carpet remnant or small rug as for children to sit while they "stop and think" about their choices.
- Purchase a simple and inexpensive count-down timer with a bell for timing reasonable completion of requests and time out sessions.
- Sterilize (remove) from the children's rooms anything considered a privilege and that cannot be managed while they are in the room during shut-down.
- Use the Texas Three-Step (1, 2, 3, E.B.T.) System.

1. Make eye contact and give a reasonable request with the reasonable time to complete the request. Set the timer for the chosen time. Walk away.

2. Return when the timer goes off. If the child complied with the request, thank and compliment for the cooperation. If the child did not comply, call for the carpet and set time for two minutes for a stop and think about their choice session. Walk away. When the timer rings, return and ask the child to complete

the original request and reduce the time for completion that you originally gave for the task, but make it reasonable. Set the timer to that time and walk away. When the timer rings, return. If the child has complied, thank and compliment for the cooperation.

3. If the child has chosen not to comply, instate the E.B.T., which has been earned. The child is now on "shut-down" and will not have access to any earned privileges until the debt is paid off and the child begins to cooperate with requests and rules.

- An E.B.T. is either 30 minutes or an hour earlier to bed, with the lights off. This must be voluntary. That is, it is the child's choice whether or not to comply. When the child does this successfully, the shut-down status is returned to full "go status" in the morning. The child once again has access to all privileges.
- Honor the child's choice and do not coerce or force the E.B.T.

Chapter 14: The Hybrid

- An E.B.T. can be issued immediately, without going through the steps. This should be used only for behaviors that are dangerous or ones that violate family values (disrespect, cursing, destroying property, lying, stealing, etc.). This tactic should not be overused or it will be perceived as controlling and punitive.
- The goal is to become a natural teacher by using natural and logical consequences.
- Set reasonable, logical, and natural limits and remain consistent. A child who is determined to oppose

reasonable limits and systems of managing behavior is choosing to not be a member of the family team.
- Power parents are left with two options: Honor the child's choice and find a suitable place for him/her to live or attempt to force the child to be on the team and live with the associated chaos and destruction.
- When a child becomes proficient in the 1, 2, 3, E.B.T. System, we can use a slight, but effective variation: 1, 2, 3, A.C.T. It is the same system with the substitution of an Alternative Chore Time for the Early Bed Time.
- One A.C.T. is equal to either 30 minutes or one hour of an "Alternative Chore." The child would choose from a menu of several tasks or chores that would benefit the family. These chores would take 30 minutes to an hour to complete and must be done well.

Chapter 15: One-Way Trip with Our Memories Meter Ticking

- Our goal as power parents is to generate at least a two-to-one ratio of good memories versus bad memories.
- Creativity will generate a plethora of positive memories.
- Our legacy is to leave our self with our children and grandchildren.
- The journey can be enjoyable and exciting.
- Corrections along the way may be needed to stay on course.
- All of our values and principles, all of our tenderness and encouragement, all of our love and goodness will be passed on generation after generation through our children.
- Sweet memories are the paradise of our minds.

A Personal Message

YOU ARE TO be congratulated for choosing to become a power parent by claiming not only your rights, but the rights of your children. As a result of your commitment, your children, their children, and progeny for generations to come will remain focused on the unalienable rights and principles that guide us to self-regulation and happiness.

Regardless of the plethora of technological advances and external pressures that tend to disintegrate families, your efforts will *empower* your family. All healthy governments and societies depend on the family as the central agency for everything that is good in people.

I wish you the very best as you steadfastly remain committed to your exciting and rewarding journey. Make it the best you can and enjoy the process. You will make a difference in our society that only "*you*" can make. Your children need you to be powerful and effective parents. Claim *Your* power and expand *Your* dreams.

Your viewpoints of this power parent process are important to me. Please share your successes or difficulties by contacting me at http://www.thepower-parent.com, where you will find more ideas and support.

—Dr. B

THE END

Appendix
Child and caregiver behavior patterns before the age of 18 months

Attachment Pattern - Secure

Child
Uses caregiver as a secure base for exploration. Protests caregiver's departure and seeks proximity and is comforted on return, returning to exploration. May be comforted by the stranger, but shows clear preference for the caregiver.

Caregiver
Responds appropriately, promptly and consistently to needs. Caregiver has successfully formed a secure parental attachment bond to the child.

Attachment Pattern - Avoidant

Child
Little affective sharing in play. Little or no distress on departure, little or no visible response to return, ignoring or turning away with no effort to maintain contact if picked up. Treats the stranger similarly to the caregiver. The child feels that there is no attachment; therefore, the child is rebellious and has a lower self-image and self-esteem.

Caregiver
Little or no response to distressed child. Discourages crying and encourages independence.

Attachment Pattern – Ambivalent/Anxious or Resistant

Child
Unable to use caregiver as a secure base, seeking proximity before separation occurs. Distressed on separation with ambivalence, anger, reluctance to warm to caregiver and return to play. Preoccupied with caregiver's availability, seeking contact but resisting angrily when it is achieved. Not easily calmed by stranger. In this relationship, the child always feels anxious because the caregiver's availability is never consistent.

Caregiver
Inconsistent between appropriate and neglectful responses. Generally will only respond after increased attachment behavior from the infant.

Attachment Pattern - Disorganized

Child
Stereotyped behavior on return, such as freezing or rocking. Lack of coherent attachment strategy shown by contradictory, disoriented behaviors, such as approaching, but with the back turned.

Caregiver
Frightened or frightening behavior, intrusiveness, withdrawal, negativity, role confusion, affective communication errors and maltreatment. Very often associated with many forms of abuse towards the child.